# Mthers

## OF THE

# Village

Published by Familius LLC, www.familius.com
Familius books are available at special discounts for bulk purchases, whether for sales
promotions or for family or corporate use. For more information, contact Familius Sales at
559-876-2170 or email orders@familius.com.

Library of Congress Cataloging-in-Publication Data
2015955956

Print ISBN 9781942934370
Ebook ISBN 9781942934882
Hardcover ISBN 9781942934899

Printed in the United States of America

Edited by Michele Robbins and Lindsay Sandberg
Cover Design by David Miles
Book Design by Lindsay Sandberg

10 9 8 7 6 5 4 3 2 1
First Edition

# M*o*thers
## OF THE
# Village

Why All Moms Need the Support of
a Motherhood Community
and How to Find It for Yourself

C . J . SCHNEIDER

For my mom, who passed on her love of reading and of being a mother.

For my dad, who taught me how to find the humor in even the toughest patches of life.

For my husband, who I make music and babies and chaos with.

And for my children, who have my heart entirely.

# Contents

# Part I

# Why a Village?

My intent in writing this book is to offer hope and encouragement to all of those looking to strengthen their own networks of support and improve the quality of their motherhood experience. It is not to discourage mothers suffering from postpartum depression from seeking professional help.

My objective is to give moms options for how they can improve their mothering experience, lighten their own loads, and find joy in connecting with other moms. Being a part of a mothering village can help moms be more resilient and better equipped to overcome depression, fatigue, loneliness, anger, and guilt.

In sharing my own experiences with village building, along with the experiences of other mothers who have also shared their inspiring stories, I hope to offer useful ideas of how to build the villages we all need.

# CHAPTER 1

# My Story

Eight months after giving birth to my third child, I found myself sitting in front of my doctor talking about the side effects of antidepressants. She wrote out a prescription; I got it filled, went home, and set the pill bottle in my cupboard.

As I placed the pills down, still not quite believing that it had come to this, I looked at my antidepressants and sadly thought to myself, "Well, there's my community." The reason why the word *community* came to my mind first—before any other word, such as *happiness* or *sanity*—was because, besides being completely sleep deprived, the most overwhelming feeling that drove me to the doctor's office in the first place was loneliness.

My loneliness was often manifested in bursts of frustration and anger. Once, shortly before my visit to the doctor, I went grocery shopping with my baby girl and toddler son. I was exhausted and grumpy, my shopping list was long, and, after undergoing the trials of shopping with two small children, I was relieved when I finally reached the checkout line. I reached into my bag to pull out my wallet only to realize that I had left it in my van. I took a deep breath and pushed the heavy cart over to one of the store's greeters. I explained the situation and asked if I could please take the loaded cart—with my children strapped in—out to the parking lot to quickly get my wallet and then come back to pay. The older gentleman shook his head. No. There was no way they could let me do that. It was, of course, against store policy. An understandable position for anyone who isn't stark raving mad. I, however, *was* stark raving mad. So when the greeter told me I had to take my cranky, tired kids out of the cart and haul them in my weary arms to my van, what lit my chest on fire was not the effort ahead of me but the message I felt was being delivered: I really was on my own, and not even the paid door greeter at Walmart would help me.

And so, with my fuse lit, I began, right there in the store, to angrily unload all of the groceries from the cart onto the floor right beside that well-intentioned, bewildered greeter.

I have been known to possess a natural flair for the dramatic, even before children entered the scene, but the grocery store incident was definitely out of character for me. The signs were all there: I had acclimated to feeling miserable all the time and was disconnected from myself physically and emotionally. I ignored flu-like symptoms and joint pain, I stopped feeling happy *or* sad, and I couldn't stop eating—picture a bleary-eyed Godzilla in Candyland.

I needed some help.

I needed my village.

I haven't always craved a close community in such a desperate way. Before having kids, I was a pretty independent person. I've never had a difficult time leaving people or places behind, because I naturally delight in the novelty of change. For many years, I didn't really think that having a solid, consistent community was all that important. Perhaps it is because, for most of my life, I have found ready connections and been able to develop meaningful friendships fairly easily. However, this ease in building a new community became progressively harder as I started having children. Shocking how no one wants to cozy up to the strange, crazy lady who looks like she is ready—even eager—to step into an Ultimate Fighting Championship ring at a moment's notice.

Now that I look back at my life, I see how important community has been all along. I guess I just took it for granted. I can now see that at every stage of my adult life, I have benefited tremendously from being a part of a community.

During my university studies, I lived in a house full of students which we named The Pit. It lived up to its name. It was old, gross, neglected, and cheap. That run-down place (which I would shudder at living in now) holds some of my favorite memories, because I had good, solid friends there—a community, a group of girls with whom I could talk about my life and my worries. We did Tae Bo in our living room, shared ideas about art, took road trips, and listened to a lot of Neil Diamond together.

I also found community through joining the Canadian Naval Reserves to help pay for a semester abroad in Amsterdam. I struggled through boot camp and am so glad I did, because that experience helped me see the importance of group cohesion and demonstrated the powerful force that can be created when people organize and work together toward a common goal. I loved the feeling of knowing that my platoon had my back and shared the understanding that "you are only as fast as your slowest man."

After university, I put a plane ticket to Taiwan on my credit card and taught English for a year and a half. I lived with two other women who were definitely kindred spirits. The best memories I have of Taiwan are of the people I connected with who loved me, laughed with me, and taught me. Although I can happily recount the joys that friendship and connection brought me in the past, it has taken me a while to truly understand and appreciate what deep and meaningful connections really look like.

While I was living in Taipei, I met Jackie, an experienced mother of five who shared with me a heartwarming example of a connection she had made in her own life. I count her as one of my teachers even though it took years for me to be able to look back and finally benefit from her wisdom.

In Taipei, I was a leader of a church youth group. Jackie was one of the other leaders. She was concerned about a young Taiwanese woman who wanted to join what was a mostly American, English-speaking youth group. Jackie wanted to talk with the girls about being inclusive and helping the Taiwanese girl feel loved, appreciated, and part of the group, but I had reservations. I told her that maybe the girl would feel more comfortable in a group that spoke her language. Although she could speak some English, irony, cultural references, and humor were difficult for her to grasp. It was beyond me how they would be able to truly connect and find common ground with such communication barriers.

Jackie, however, shared a different view. Her husband was an international pilot, so they had lived in many different places all over the world. When they lived in China, they had already started their family and found themselves without relatives or a community. She was very much on her own with the exception of her hired help, a Chinese woman named Mei, who helped her look after her babies and her home. She recounted with emotion and love how much she cherished Mei. Their friendship didn't develop because they loved the same books or had the same political views or both religiously followed Neil Diamond's career. They had a deep connection because they washed floors together and played and cared for babies together—Mei was there for Jackie during a difficult and lonely time.

I often think of Jackie's story and am grateful to her for helping shape the way I approach connecting with others as a mother. However, when I was living in Taiwan, I had never experienced friendship like that before. Before I had children, I didn't fully understand the camaraderie that can come from working with someone through hard times; my community was largely constructed around pleasure and fun. I just didn't get it.

I *really* didn't get it.

When I had moved back to Edmonton (after living in Taiwan), during a horrible Canadian spring when there was still snow on the ground, I took time off from work and drove down to California to visit a friend I'd made when we were both in Taiwan. She had a baby, maybe a year old, who was born with a condition that required intensive mothering. My friend was an angel mother to her son, who the doctors predicted wouldn't live long after birth. She loved that boy so much I think her love kept him alive. I appreciate all of this now. She is a hero to me.

But when I visited her, I was clueless and selfish. I loved the benefits of connectedness but had no interest in the work it requires. I remember hitting California and thinking that all I wanted to do was go surfing. I met up with my friend and, of course, she had this baby and couldn't go surfing. I can distinctly remember feeling annoyed that this baby was in the way of our fun. Every time I think about this, my chest burns with shame. But that was me—I loved my freedom and independence. I hadn't yet moved on from the youthful idea that my needs and personal fulfillment should always come first.

My lack of perspective was compounded with the fact that I don't naturally love to commit. To anything. I like different and new, and the idea of an extended period of sameness makes me feel a little claustrophobic. I'm not great at staying in one place and worse at keeping in touch with those I've left behind. Even desirables, like having a solid career and marriage and settling down, frightened me. Quite frankly, the importance of community was completely lost on me. I didn't think I needed it. I was independent—I had a job, a car, and a good amount of vacation days. I didn't like the idea of being tied down to anyone or anything.

A large part of me loved the freedom I had at that time. However, every so often, in a quiet moment, I began to feel restlessness in my heart. I could sense that I was missing something. While at first my heart delivered those messages in quiet moments, eventually it started throwing temper tantrums. That bossy little heart of mine kept nagging at me; it needed more than what I was offering. The message was clear—it needed someone else to love.

I remembered being taught by my parents and my religion that commitment to family was a gateway to deep and lasting joy. My heart desperately wanted all of the happiness, wisdom, strength, and power that I was told could come my way by having a family. Although all of this business of commitment, of showing up and being consistent and dependable in a family, was not naturally what I would have gone for, I thought it was time to try giving up something good for something better. It seemed to be exactly the thing my heart had been pining for.

I married my husband, Jordan, fairly close to home, and two days later we boarded an airplane and left for the UK. We landed in Oxford, where he studied and I worked. We met many couples from all over who were eager to connect, explore, and have fun. I remember an impromptu camping trip, frequent dinners at a beloved, cozy English restaurant, and going to the theater whenever we felt like it. It was heaven; my gamble had paid off.

And then I got pregnant—I reached for the apple and was cast out of Eden.

Becoming a mother changes everything. With each child I had, I became more vulnerable and more desperate for a village.

I had two sons three years apart while we were living in Scotland. My first, Will, slowed us down a bit, but we were still relatively unencumbered. During my days at home, I would put Will in the BabyBjörn and go walking on a beautiful little trail that ran along the Scottish countryside. On weekends, we would drive an hour or so even farther into the country and hike for hours with Will on Jordan's back.

My parents came to visit and took us on a trip around Europe. We rented a car and brought a stroller. Will, a year and a half old, was content to sit in his stroller while we wheeled him around Germany, Austria, Croatia, Italy, and Slovenia.

When I was pregnant with my second child, my husband's parents came to visit and took us to Portugal. Not only was I uncomfortably pregnant (cue foreboding music), but Will was now a toddler and had no interest in staying in his stroller. Of course, being in Portugal was great, but there was something so frustrating about being in a place that begged to be explored only to have to spend the entire time in a cloud of pregnancy misery, chasing after a toddler who insisted on napping our afternoons away. He seemed to only care about chasing pigeons or butterflies and had no interest in art, architecture, or culture (two-year-olds can be so weird like that). On that trip, I was confronted with the realization that motherhood, although not overwhelming at that point, was definitely getting trickier.

It wasn't just getting trickier logistically, but financially as well. Although our parents had the resources to help us do some traveling, the reality of day-to-day living was financially strenuous—we had to buy groceries with our credit cards at times. To further complicate things, my husband was nervous about possibly losing his job, as were many others I knew, when the 2008 recession hit. It was a time when a woman needed some sisters.

Fortunately, that is exactly what I had. Nestled in our little Scottish community of Peterculter was a mom-and-tots group. I began attending and connected with a wonderful group of moms from around the world. We all had two things in common: we all had toddlers and most of us lived very far from family.

Outside of the moms' group, we had play dates, went on walks, and celebrated birthdays and Christmas (even though one mom was Buddhist and another was married to a Muslim). I cherished my friendship with those women, who often felt like family. We experienced our "firsts" together and shared tips on potty training, birthing techniques, cooking, discipline tactics, and teething.

When I became pregnant with my second baby and I had less to offer in terms of personality and energy, my friendships deepened with the other mamas in my life. As I made my way from my first child to my second, I began to understand what all those people yakking about community were saying.

Three of those mothers in particular generously taught me about village living. When I was heavily pregnant with my second and struggling, one of my dear friends came to my little flat with cleaning supplies and her children. She cheerily announced that I was free to go take a nap while she kept an eye on my son. I went into my room and lay down while she and her older children cleaned my apartment. I felt overwhelmed with gratitude. Years later, as I think about that day, my heart warms with a fierce love for that woman. It wasn't the childcare; it wasn't the nap; it wasn't the clean flat (although those things were lovely). It was that this woman showed up, busy as she was, and let me know that I wasn't alone.

I had another dear friend who—despite my slow, foggy, grumpy self—kept inviting me out for walks along beautiful Scottish trails and around peaceful castle gardens. I don't know how I would have survived that time without her.

Another friend, a woman from Mexico who lived in Aberdeen with her husband and little girl, was always so generous with her food, her home, and her friendship. Many times she mentioned how lonely she felt in Aberdeen. Where she was from in Mexico, friends and family would drop by unannounced all the time. They would come by and ask to use the shower or return something borrowed or sit down for a little chat. Her home in Mexico was openly connected to the lives of others.

The openness of Mexico was a distant dream in the reserved UK, so one year for her birthday I thought of organizing people to show up at her home unannounced every hour for random reasons but I chickened out—those worlds were so different. I thought people would think I was strange. I now wish I had made a different choice. Maybe people *would* have thought I was a weirdo—maybe no one would have agreed to do it because it would have felt too strange to them. But there are a few other maybes kicking around. Maybe I would have asked some other women who were also lonely and in need of connecting with someone else. And maybe it would have recharged their souls to help another sister feel that she wasn't alone. Maybe it would have

recharged my own soul. Maybe it would have been awkward, yet deeply satisfying for everyone. It takes courage to be vulnerable, and sometimes reaching
out means you have to be a little brave. Asking for friendship and closeness
can be scary and sometimes painful, especially when your open heart meets
rejection—but not asking is ultimately worse.

It took a third baby in a new city to help me clearly see that a support
network is not just a luxury but a vital necessity and solid answer to many
problems modern parents face. According to the World Health Organization "[A lack of] social support is a relatively potent risk factor for postpartum depression."[1] A lack of social support is also a risk factor for addiction,
mental health problems, poor health, slower rehabilitation, and many other
problems. This is not just true for moms—social support is an irreplaceable
existential need that everyone has. And there are times when we feel this truth
more desperately, times when we are more vulnerable to the effects of loneliness. This was the case for me when I became pregnant with my third baby.

Looking back, I can clearly see that I had stumbled into the middle of a
perfect storm. The conditions required for any mama to lose her marbles
were, like some grand, unfortunate miracle, all there.

I love my children with a white-hot kind of love. However, I hate, with all
the dark fire of Hades, how I feel when I am pregnant. I would rather give
birth every month for nine months than be pregnant for the same amount of
time. And my third pregnancy was the worst. It made Basic Military Training
seem like an obstacle course at the local playground. In addition to being
ridiculously miserable, I was also exhausted, huge, and doing my best to care
for two other kids.

Jordan, our two sons, and I returned to Canada in the middle of a Canadian winter after living in the relatively balmy UK for five years. The climate
did nothing to help me forge connections. During Canadian winters, when
you open your door to the outside world, there is a blast of cold that tries to
bully you into staying inside. Inside and alone.

We also jumped around different neighborhoods for the first two years we
were back. And just before we moved into our new house, I became pregnant
with my third child. I didn't know a single neighbor. My husband worked
very long hours and, when he wasn't at work, he was involved in the running

of our home. I could see that things were tough for him at that time too; he was tired and stretched, but he still did the laundry, took the kids to the park, and stepped up in countless other ways. We have always loved each other's company and have always been great friends, but we needed more than just each other—most couples do.

As much as I needed other women in my life, I couldn't seem to get myself to the community mom-and-tots group. I tried to make friends with parents from school, but I am only now, a couple of years later, reaping the fruit of hellos said and labored smiles given. And although I attended a church where there were women who did their best to reach out to me, I just couldn't seem to reach back. I was counting down the days to when my baby would be born and I could finally start to live a real life again.

When Sadie was finally born, I felt euphoric over the fact that I had my body to myself again. I was pretty happy for the first few months and felt quite hopeful that I would leave my unhappiness behind.

But Sadie just would *not* sleep. She would wake up so many times during the night that in the morning all I had the energy and motivation to do was turn on cartoons for my toddler and slog inelegantly through the day. I didn't have the luxury of an afternoon nap as I had with my first, because my middle son wasn't napping anymore and Sadie's naps seemed to only last forty-five minutes. This went on for eight months, and then I became so exhausted that I just kind of lost my mind.

I became overly anxious and, even though I was desperate for rest, when the day was over and it was time to go to bed, my mind raced and worried about inconsequential matters. I couldn't sleep, so I stayed up, watching movies long into the night. Quite predictably, I crashed. I crashed and, with two active boys and a baby, I didn't have the time or mental resources to climb back up.

There were acquaintances who offered help, but I didn't even know what to ask for. How do you ask for a sound night's sleep when you're breastfeeding? How do you ask someone you barely know to take all of your children for a week—maybe even a month—while you take the time to get right? So I just kept plodding through my days, angry and impatient, not really wanting to connect with anyone and mostly just wanting to be left alone.

What I really needed was to *not* be left alone. I needed community, I needed family, I needed lifelong friends to come and cry with me, tell me jokes, and watch my kids regularly while I went outside for fresh air and exercise.

But I didn't have any of that nearby. I hadn't stayed in one place long enough to build a support system. And so I went to the doctor, who was, unfortunately, unable to prescribe a close-knit sisterhood of women who lived communally and whose daily rhythms and tasks were interwoven and dependent on one another. That's what I wish she could have handed me before she wrote a prescription for those little white pills.

To be clear, I am not writing this book as an attempt to discourage mothers from seeking professional help or from taking medication to deal with post-partum depression. Ultimately, this book isn't about postpartum depression at all. The hardships of mothering are not limited to pregnancy or labor or the postpartum period. Although those may be particularly vulnerable times, the truth is that, while children bring amazing wonder and joy, raising them can also open unimaginable doors of heartache and struggle. We all need backup when we take on the task of ushering little ones through this life. This book is meant to create a space for us mothers to consider our networks of support with the hope that, as we consider our experiences as mothers, we will be fruitful in creating more supportive environments for ourselves and for the next generation of girls who will one day become mothers themselves.

This is the understanding I have arrived at: that our fates as mothers are tied together, and our collective hardships and heartbreaks are infinitely better and more healthily managed when weathered together.

In the summer of 1890, Vincent Van Gogh finished "Wheatfield with Crows," one of the last paintings he would work on before the end of his life on July 29, 1890. Half of the painting is of a golden, bountiful wheat field. Above the happy harvest hangs a dark, foreboding sky. A storm is brewing. The scene seems a perfect painting of motherhood, with its golden joys tied to a frequently stormy sky. And when the skies are stormy and the thunder booms (as it will in every mother's journey), I am saddened that all too often in our modern, busy, liberated world, so many mothers walk the path alone.

If you look closely at Van Gogh's paintings, you will see hundreds of little brush strokes. Hundreds of brush strokes unite on his canvases to create a picture and tell a story. None of these strokes could sit singly on some other blank canvas and tell the same powerful story on their own. Like Van Gogh's painting, the great creative work we women are all part of—the work of taking care of the next generation—is a story that needs many brush strokes, side-by-side, in order to turn out to be a true masterpiece.

Motherhood in this age—where women are so disconnected from one another that natural resources of help and support do not ubiquitously exist—is a breeding ground for insanity. Mothers are not meant to act as single brush strokes. We are not at our collective best when we separate ourselves. Mothers are meant to unite.

# ENDNOTES

1.   Emma Robertson et al., "Risk Factors for Postpartum Depression," in Donna E. Stewart et al., *Postpartum Depression: Literature Review of Risk Factors and Interventions* (Toronto: University Health Network Women's Health Program, 2003).

# CHAPTER 2

# Keeping Company with Anger and Guilt

Do you imagine the universe is agitated? Go into the desert at night and look out at the stars. This practice should answer the question.
—Lao Tzu

Can we do that here? In our imaginations? Let's imagine we step out into the brisk, desert night air. Barely able to see the sand your next step will land on, you stop, and as you feel the vastness and stillness overwhelm you, your eyes are led upward by the tantalizing sparkle of the star-studded sky. As you look up into the miracle of infinity before you, your mind suddenly remembers that you forgot to call the school to let them know you couldn't help out with that field trip after all. . . . Speaking of field trips, did my husband sign the consent form or did I? I can't believe I have to sign all of those permission slips, even for a simple science presentation in the gym. Why does life have to be so busy and complicated?

And then, there it is. Back at the car, your kids are impatiently honking the horn to summon you so they can recount the excruciating minutia of the argument they just had, and also, the littlest one has just pooped her pants. Again. And you're alone, in the desert, with your smelly, crying kids. Do you look up again and resent the stars for having such a cushy place to rest? Maybe Lao Tzu should have spent less time hanging out in the desert and more time at home helping out with the kids. I don't know. But when I think about the hard time after my third child was born, I vividly recall feeling agitated—all of the time. I wasn't even close to feeling at one with some peaceful desert night sky.

I'm not the only mama out there who has had those feelings. Anger and guilt are both getting in the way of our desert-night-sky bliss. First, though, we must be willing to look those two thugs—anger and guilt—squarely in the eye before we can tell them to take a hike.

## Embracing Truth Telling, Mess and All

Before I get into anger and guilt, I want to use a little space here to make a case for why it's important to talk about the tough and tricky parts of living.

I have always been a fan of embracing the good, the bad, and the ugly. So after my doctor handed me the prescription for some antidepressants, I was ready to figure my misery out. For company and clarity, I dove into mom literature and found compatible companions—mothers writing their way through their sadness and anger in an attempt to make sense of it all. Reading books like *The Price of Motherhood, Perfect Madness: Motherhood in the Age of Insanity*, and *The Bitch in the House* helped me feel a little less crazy, or at least established for me that crazy, sadly enough, just might be the norm.

Some women hate these kinds of books because they seem whiny, indulgent, ungrateful, negative, and angry. I would agree that there are times in life when you must accept your lot, suck it up, soldier on, and appreciate that struggles can make us more beautiful human beings—I think motherhood has always offered that. Motherhood has always been fraught with challenge and pain and anguish alongside the joy, love, and fulfillment.

In fact, motherhood and suffering have been offered as a package deal since the beginning. In the Judeo-Christian account of Adam and Eve, Mother Eve was told by God, "In sorrow thou shalt bring forth children."[1] I don't think he was condemning; I think he was explaining.

The suffering and sacrifice that motherhood demands is universal. There are mothers in North Korea who have to watch their children starve to death; mothers who lose their children to child armies in Africa; mothers who are pushed by poverty to send their daughters to work in brothels; climate-change refugee mothers who must leave their homes and are forced to raise their children in slums; mothers in Burma who lose their children because they cannot afford TB medicine.

My story of exhaustion and isolation may not seem very problematic to many, especially when compared with these examples. However, at the heart of all of the hardships I mention, including my own, there *is* one common thread: a painful disconnection from the people they love. It is a difficult blow. It is a blow that can make life seem as though it is not worth living, because being connected with others is a basic human need. This isn't some whiny first-world problem—this is the stuff of basic survival.

During harsh times, though counterintuitive, suffering can be an instrument of joy, because it facilitates our essential need to feel valued and loved by other people. In my own suffering, I have seen how the love I had for my mother grew and grew when my mother came to me during some dark days and helped me in a way no one else had or even could have. And when a woman invited me into her home and into her life, even though I had little to give back at that time, my heart developed a fierce loyalty and love for her. And when my husband plodded through life with my angry, sad, horrible self with patience and love and commitment, my love for him was cemented.

Human suffering has the potential to unite. In suffering, there is opportunity for courage and great love and sacrifice and realizing that we all need each other—a great reminder of our interconnectedness. Sharing the pains and heartaches of motherhood can be great connecting experiences. I see the offering of a woman to be willing to "mourn with those who mourn"[2] as a positive, connecting, and loving act. And we, as mothers, have many opportunities to mourn together.

It seems, though, that we have largely retreated from that communal, shared, connected way of mothering. I believe that devastating disconnect is playing a major role in bringing an unhealthy, unproductive type of suffering to mothers, fathers, and children today. When strength-building troubled waters become overwhelming, crushing tsunamis, then it's time to move from where we are and go in search of higher ground.

We mothers need to figure out how to connect our lives and our hearts with each other. To do this we need to recognize that *truth telling helps love to flourish*. We need to be able to open up to each other honestly and without feeling the pressure to pretend that our lives are practically perfect in every way.

There is a massively powerful idea floating around that positivity trumps all. I know that positivity in the form of hope and gratitude and love are essential to our happiness—but we must also be fiercely honest with ourselves. It seems as though we have to keep reminding each other of the value of being open and honest, and I think a big part of why we do this is because many people only want to hear the good, the happy, the fluff, the pink, the sunshine stories. We don't want downers. But the price we pay is that we miss valuable truths, honest hearts, and sincere pleas for help. When you lie to yourself and refuse to acknowledge stories of truth (yours and others'), you are actively disconnecting from yourself and from others. By denying a problem, you are also the furthest you could be from ever finding a solution.

Truth connects.

It enlightens.

It is the path to freedom.

My favorite part of Steinbeck's *East of Eden* is when Lee's father tells him the horrific story of how his mother died. Lee recounts:

> And when my father would tell me [the story] I would say to him,
> 'Get to that lake—get my mother there—don't let it happen again,
> not this time. Just once let's tell it: how you got to the lake and built a
> house of fir boughs.' And my father became very Chinese then. He
> said, 'There's more beauty in the truth even if it is dreadful beauty.
> The storytellers at the city gate twist life so that it looks sweet to
> the lazy and the stupid and the weak, and this only strengthens their
> infirmities and teaches nothing, cures nothing, nor does it let the
> heart soar.'[3]

Regardless of circumstance, our anger and guilt are always important matters of consequence. While it might be tempting to trivialize anger and guilt (or berate ourselves for feeling them in the first place), we should remind ourselves that hard and ugly things have the potential to unite us with our community and help our hearts to soar.

# Opting Out of Motherhood

As I was sitting with a bank manager one day, applying for a credit card and talking about switching banks, this book came into the conversation. The man seemed intrigued. It's possible his interest was feigned, as he was hoping to persuade me to switch banks; however, he did share something that seemed quite genuine. He said that his fiancée seemed to show no interest in having kids, an attitude very unlike his very loving and very involved mother. To her (and to a lot of his friends), having children meant closing a lot of doors. Career doors, finance doors, vacation doors, freedom doors. The story seemed to be: *and then they had children . . . which was the end of them.* I can't help but think how backward that is, because I know deep down that my children were the beginning of me in so many ways, and that they have opened emotional and spiritual doors for me that never would have opened without them. Still, I can certainly understand how women look at the mess of motherhood and hesitate a little.

Yet there is more than just hesitation on the rise. A small but increasing number of moms are abandoning their children and family altogether.

In a CNN opinion piece, Peggy Drexler writes about the seeming rise in mothers who abandon their families.

> Most mothers are familiar with the feeling—for some it's more fleeting than for others—of total exhaustion, frustration, a sense of being overwhelmed by duty and the responsibility of raising children. Maybe some indulge in a momentary fantasy of running away.
>
> Though there are no hard numbers, reports would seem to indicate that the number of moms who actually do run away—or at least walk away—is increasing . . . Anecdotally, too, we're hearing more from mothers who leave their children due to choice or circumstance.[4]

Drexler states that the increasing number of walk-away mothers may be because we are living in an increasingly self-centered culture that values and supports people who make choices that are good for themselves individually and momentarily, regardless of the consequences to other people or society in general. While I see her point and do agree that the glorification of individuality is causing problems in many people's lives, I wonder if it's also true that many mothers are simply in desperate need of love, support, and a strong community, and when they live without that, those mothers are opting out, falling apart, and running away.

A severe case of an unsupported woman—a person who desperately needed community—occurred in July 2013. A woman from Winnipeg, Manitoba, drowned her two-year-old daughter and three-month-old son in the bathtub and then killed herself. Photos of her show a pretty woman with blonde curls framing her smiling face. Others show her smiling while holding her newborn son with her sweet daughter cozied up to her on the couch.[5]

Although the mother involved in this incident was suffering from postpartum psychosis rather than postpartum depression, the incident triggered a heartfelt response online from mothers who felt this story perhaps hit a little too close to home. The news offered an opportunity for many women to speak out about their own difficult postpartum experiences. There were so many women who, under the comfort of online anonymity, shared personal moments of their own mothering experience. These comments came from moms who also needed help—a network, a backup, a community of mothers who they could rely on instead of trudging alone through their challenges feeling tired, isolated, and angry.

The incident, though an extreme example, is a striking cautionary tale of what can happen when moms do not have enough support. It is also a good reminder that although a mom may seem like the perfect picture of motherhood on the outside, there may be a storm brewing within. And from what I've seen and gathered, it seems as though there are more than a few storms brewing out there.

## Mothers in the Trenches

As I started writing a book of my own, I posted a message to my friends and family asking for stories of motherhood. As the stories came in, I began to see some common threads. The themes of loneliness, fatigue, and anger came up again and again. Here are a few stories I received from mothers in the trenches:

I am a single mom who works full-time outside of the home and then tries her best to take care of her three kids, ages five, three, and one. My two youngest girls have been sick and last night was my breaking point. I think I'm coming down with what they have had, so I was already exhausted and not feeling great by the time I got home from work. My three-year-old was using the bathroom by herself while I was trying to fix supper and pick up the house and help the oldest with his math homework.

That's when it happened. I went to check on her and found her helping the littlest use the potty, too. As I mentioned, they were both sick and the little one was on the potty, but she didn't make it all the way so there was diarrhea all over the floor (and walls). To make matters worse, my three-year-old was trying to "help clean up" by dumping an entire bottle of liquid soap onto the mess. I lost it. I sat on the floor and cried. For a long time. Finally, I had to pick myself up off of the floor. I got the mess cleaned up, burning supper in the process. I told the kids we were having cereal for supper, which they loved, and we spent the rest of the night cuddled up in my bed so that everyone could be next to mommy, and we watched movies.

I think what gets me through is knowing that I'm the only one there to do it, so it has to be done. Although, sometimes that makes the things I should be enjoying with my children much more of a chore to me.

My mom has passed away, and I don't have any girlfriends who are in my situation and can relate to what I am going through. —Jessica

From another:

When I was pregnant with my first, I was just sick all the time. My immune system went to crap so I got a lot of common colds but then those turned into strep throat, and then I got bronchitis. Twice. Bronchitis is horrible when you're pregnant because when you are pregnant, you don't really have control over your bladder the way you used to. So when I was coughing really hard—because I was nauseous and my gag reflex was really sensitive—I ended up coughing and throwing up and peeing my pants all at the same time. And that happened sometimes at work, which was really unpleasant. That happened outside of work, too. One day, I was driving to work, got three blocks, and I threw up in my car.

I was really exhausted, too. My husband was working out of town at the time. He'd be gone for four days at a time and I would just be fending for myself. I worked my day job, and then I worked evenings and weekends as well so I had very limited time and energy. I couldn't connect with anyone, I couldn't do anything, I was just so sick and exhausted that I barely made it to my doctor appointments. After work I'd just go home and cry or go to bed. I was really sad. I felt sorry for myself and wished I was my old self—full of energy and love with lots of friends.

It was hard—it was a lot harder than I thought it would be. I was withdrawn from everybody. I just couldn't do anything and after your friends keep calling you to go out and you consistently turn them down, after enough rejections, they just stop calling. It's almost as though you don't exist anymore. Not that people don't care about you anymore, it's just they don't see you or hear from you, so they continue on with their lives and you continue on with yours. —Claire

And from another:

It is frustrating to spend an hour (or even just 5 minutes) making food just to have it dumped on the floor: over and over and over again, in the same meal! There is the battle between just putting the toys away because it's faster or trying to "teach" your child to clean. There is the laundry that grows exponentially with each child. If you are lucky, it's just washable marker on the wall—not permanent marker or screwdriver carvings. All furniture, walls, and flooring will get both sticky and actually permanently damaged.

The list goes on, but it's not the length of the list, the severity of damage, or the substantial financial hit that makes *mess* so frustrating and discouraging. It's the monotony. Mothers perform the same mind numbing routines over and over and over and over. Every day, every week, every month, every year. It feels demeaning and lonely. After a world offering financial reward for effort (even monotonous jobs), awards for participation and completion, and grades for learning—your daily efforts to hold the mess at bay are rarely even noticed and never rewarded. "Unappreciated" is the simple cliché (and sounds so much like whining) but the feelings of un-fulfillment can be so much deeper. —Amy

I have felt a strange reassurance as I've read through so many stories from moms telling of their loneliness, frustration, and anger. What they offered me was a sense of relief as I came to the comforting realization, *Phew, I'm not the only one who feels this way* .

## Just File That Under Angry

For many moms, in the eye of their storm, there are the common feelings of being unsupported, unacknowledged, unheard, and unloved. In short—disconnected. To cope, we often turn this sadness into anger. Usually, it is a counterproductive tactic, because picking up a few kindred spirits when there's a whiff of anger on your every breath is generally not so easy. I was eventually able to diffuse my anger, but before I could do that I had to acknowledge my anger. Then, I had to look underneath it.

Feeling loved, supported, and heard includes an acknowledgment—socially and politically—that the work and sacrifice we offer in giving life to children is a worthy and valued endeavor. How can we take ourselves seriously if mothers are consistently getting the message that no one else does?

Ann Crittenden, former financial reporter for the *New York Times* and Pulitzer Prize nominee, notes in her book, *The Price of Motherhood*, the vital role mothers and caregivers of the young play in the functioning of a country. She illustrates that, despite their importance, caregivers are often undervalued by society at large. Crittenden writes:

> In the modern economy, two-thirds of all wealth is created by human skills, creativity, and enterprise—what is known as "human

capital." And that means parents who are conscientiously and effectively rearing children are literally, in the words of economist Shirley Burggraf, "the major wealth producers in our economy."

If human abilities are the ultimate fount of economic progress, as many economists now agree, and if those abilities are nurtured (or stunted) in the early years, then mothers and other caregivers of the young are the most important producers in the economy. They do have, literally, the most important job in the world.[6]

Despite the vital contribution to society a woman makes by becoming a mother, in many countries, respect for our work can dip dangerously low. No wonder so many women see motherhood as an ending rather than a beginning; everyone needs to feel that their contributions are valuable.

Judith Warner, author of *Perfect Madness*, wrote of the current trend of madness among mothers and noted that families break down when mothers (and fathers) feel unsupported, having to face the challenges of family life without a network of support.

Warner sat down with hundreds of women and asked them to talk about their experiences as mothers. Mostly meeting with middle and upper-middle class mothers, Warner writes that so often they would start by describing how grateful they should really be for their life situations, yet as conversations grew deeper and more personal, there seemed to be a common feeling, a "nagging sort of disaffection."[7] One woman who described her typical day of high-intensity homemaking and child-rearing complained, "By noon I'm ready for a padded cell."[8]

Warner writes:

Many women reported suffering from identity crises. They felt isolated in the suburbs, far from friends and their families, and the traditional support systems of other female relatives that their mothers had enjoyed. . . . It all reminded me a lot of Betty Friedan's *The Feminine Mystique*. The sense of waste. The diffuse dissatisfaction. The angst, hidden behind all the obsession with trivia, and the push to be perfect. And yet Friedan had been writing in the prefeminist 1960s. The solution Friedan dreamed of—that they could build their lives as they chose, become self-sufficient, and be fully self-realized human beings—had ostensibly come true for the women of my generation. Yet I saw, looking around, that the form of self-sufficiency we'd come into *wasn't* really a solution.[9]

As Warner states, it's not just the new moms, home with their babies, or the moms who are full-time caregivers who are feeling frustrated and angry. Cathi Hanauer, author of *The Bitch in the House*, writes on the genesis of her book.

> Two healthy children, a nice home, an interesting job . . . what could I possibly be mad about? And yet, mad I was.
>
> So, night after night, once the kids were asleep (sort of), I left laundry unfolded, phone calls unreturned, school forms unfilled out, and my own work undone to go online and fire furious e-mails to my friends to try to figure it out. And I began to realize something. A lot of [us] were resentful, guilty, [and] stressed out.[10]

Among her many friends who wrote back with tales of unhappiness and anger was one who wrote, "I'm fine all day at work, but as soon as I get home, I'm a horror," and from another, "I'm the bitch in the house."[11]

I could have been one of these venting moms. And I identified with how Hanauer summed up her feelings: "The bitch in the house. That's exactly how I felt. The opposite of what Virginia Woolf called The Angel in the House—but with anger to boot. Naturally, this outpouring of anger interested me . . . this seeming epidemic of female rage."[12]

An "epidemic of female rage" was what I was seeing in myself and in a lot of the other mothers I knew. The Angry Mom Club is, admittedly, not the most fun club to be a part of. It's not the kind of club where you strive to become a permanent member. However, change really does become instantly easier when you feel like you have others around who get where you're at.

I want to share with all the current members of The Angry Mom Club that I definitely get where you're at. At one point during my own dark days, I explained to my husband that when I was in Basic Military Training, the instructors yelled a lot. One clever trick they used to allow themselves to yell at full capacity—as often and as loudly as they wanted—was to use a sort of yelling shorthand. So instead of yelling, "LEFT TURN," they would yell, "EEEEFFF URN." So they would just drop off a few consonants to allow more volume produced with less effort. Also, although the yelled commands were understandable, they usually sounded muffled and as though they came from deep in the belly, like the growl of a bear—so the sound would come out nice and intimidating as well.

This, I suggested to my husband, was a technique I was considering implementing in my own parenting repertoire. It would be much easier on my vocal cords at a time when I felt like I was yelling everything from "YOU HAVE FIVE SECONDS TO GET YOUR SHOES ON!" to "PLEASE PASS THE BUTTER!"

I was joking (mostly).

If you're a mama who's feeling angry, you're not alone. But if you try to ignore your anger, you may one day find yourself standing in a pile of groceries, glaring at some random greeter while wondering, *How did I get here?*

## Decoding the Guilt and Anger

One day I was at a store with every cutting-edge mama product you would ever need: baby carriers, teething necklaces, breastfeeding bras, cover-ups, and, of course, cloth diapers. While I was there buying a baby carrier I asked the woman at the till about their cloth diapers, what she thought of them and if she used them. She *loved* them. She used them with her babies, and they were the best. They were eco-friendly, they didn't have those nasty chemicals that cause reactions or diaper rash, and they were cheaper in the long run if you used them for more than one kid.

After she had glowingly sung their praises, she lowered her voice and in that hushed voice admitted that at night, she put a non-cloth diaper on her baby just to avoid mess in her crib. Her boss wasn't there, just some other moms in the store. Really? Was that really so shameful a secret to admit? In that moment, it was clear that mothers had assigned a morality for everything from teething gel to cloth diapering.

In addition to the seemingly ubiquitous feeling of loneliness and disconnect that many mothers experience, we mothers seem to also spend a significant amount of time packing for our very un-exotic guilt trips. When I talk to other mothers, I hear their guilt. When I tell working mothers that I am a stay-at-home mom, I hear unsolicited explanations: reasons why they can't stay at home with their children, reasons why they shouldn't stay home with their children, and accounts of how their children are really thriving in day care. I don't ask for these explanations—it's none of my business. But for some reason, there is this need to explain this very private, personal, and often difficult choice. And when I talk to stay-at-home moms, there is also often guilt over not directly contributing to the household income or of allowing their brains to atrophy or of not loving being a stay-at-home mom or of not being able to keep a tidy house or of yelling at their kids too much.

Mothers are expressing feeling guilty so often that it inspired Steve Weins, author of the blog *The Actual Pastor*, to write the following:

> Let me be the one who says the following things out loud:
>
> You are not a terrible parent if you can't figure out a way for your children to eat as healthy as your friend's children do. She's obviously using a bizarre and probably illegal form of hypnotism.
>
> You are not a terrible parent if you yell at your kids sometimes. You have little dictators living in your house. If someone else talked to you like that, they'd be put in prison.
>
> You are not a terrible parent if you can't figure out how to calmly give them appropriate consequences in real time for every single act of terrorism that they so creatively devise.
>
> You are not a terrible parent if you'd rather be at work.
>
> You are not a terrible parent if you just can't wait for them to go to bed.
>
> You are not a terrible parent if the sound of their voices sometimes makes you want to drink and never stop.
>
> You're not a terrible parent.[13]

Maybe it feels good to hear over and over that you are not a terrible parent, but sometimes I think the conditions in which women are mothering are almost designed for failure. A man I respect once remarked that he couldn't remember his mother ever raising her voice to him. When I think of that, I wonder if she was mute. But then I remember that he grew up on a farm over eighty years ago, and he roamed free outside of his home. My own parents recall similar childhoods where days were spent freely and interactions with parents came at supper time. My husbands' parents were raised the same way—his mom was no exception, even though she was raised in the city.

Those mothers mothered decades ago.

Parenting has radically changed. Just last year, a Texas mom had police show up at her door because a neighbor complained that she was being negligent for allowing her preteen children to ride their unmotorized scooters around the cul-de-sac. She was charged with negligence. We can't let go of our children, we have to be with them *all the time*, which seems for many to be a ticking time bomb. This has not always been the case for mothers.

> Before WWII, families were mostly together all day. Moms were *doing* things with their kids. But not Legos. They were tilling the fields while the kids played nearby. They were cooking the meals with the grandmas and the aunts while the kids were in eyesight or earshot. This whole concept of a big house alone with your kids goes against all of our natural instincts that date back to caveman days/the beginning of time.[14]

So, we're all tired of feeling so guilty about everything. And some women just want to retreat from the whole thing, throw up their hands, and reject the guilt. This is probably a healthy move for many, if not most of us, right now.

But I can't help but wonder if our collective guilt isn't just maybe trying to point us in a different direction. A friend of mine uses the phrase *decode the guilt*, because guilt is, in her words, "a decoy emotion." I'm not talking about guilt over using the wrong kind of teething gel; I'm talking about a mass of mothers who know somewhere deep inside that their mothering experience could be richer somehow.

I have had the unfortunate experience of living with a seized muscle and a pinched nerve in my upper back, which persisted for over a month. It was awful. But it was also a learning process for me as I learned a lot about the usefulness of pain. Pain communicates a problem. That's all. Pain says, "Hey, stop moving around because you're making things worse." It says, "Slow down, simplify, and be careful, because that's what your body needs for you to do in order to heal." It also says, "Just call a neighbor when you lock yourself out of your house instead of climbing a ladder to the roof of your shed and crawling through your bathroom window." Pain is your body's voice.

I think guilt works a lot like pain. If the true purpose of guilt is to simply give us human beings a heads-up when we are headed down a path that is leading away from true joy, health, and harmony, then maybe our collective guilt is trying to tell us mothers that we could all use a little course correction. I think our collective guilt and anger is an important red flag. So many mothers are feeling like something is just not right, something is out of joint, something is missing. And maybe the truth is that we're all just missing each other.

# ENDNOTES

1.  Genesis 3:16 (King James Version).

2.  Romans 12:15 (New International Version).

3.  John Steinbeck, *East of Eden*, 360.

4.  Peggie Drexler, "Why There Are More Walk-Away Moms." CNN, May 6, 2013, http://www.cnn.com/2013/05/04/opinion/ drexler-mothers-leaving/.

5.  Tamara Forlanski and Lara Schroeder, "Lisa Gibson Drowned Her Children and Took Her Own Life: Police," Global News, October 4, 2013, http://globalnews.ca/news/880180/ police-classify-case-of-gibson-mom-kids-a-homicide/.

6.  Anne Crittenden, *The Price of Motherhood* (New York: Metropolitan Books, 2001), 2.

7.  Judith Warner, *Perfect Madness: Motherhood in the Age of Anxiety* (New York: Riverhead Trade, 2005), 12.

8.  Ibid., 35.

9.  Ibid., 12–13.

10. Cathi Hanauer, *The Bitch in the House: 26 Women Tell the Truth About Sex, Solitude, Work, Motherhood, and Marriage* (New York: Harper Collins Publishers, 2013), ii.

11. Ibid.,

12. Ibid.,

13. Steve Wiens, "To Parents of Small Children: Let Me Be the One Who Says It Out Loud," *The Actual Pastor* (blog), March 12, 2013, http://www.stevewiens.com/2013/03/12/ to-parents-of-small-children-let-me-be-the-one-who-says-it-out-loud/.

14. Cordes, Jill. "The Mom Mystique." *Parents*, August 16, 2013. http://www. parents.com/blogs/fearless-feisty-mama/2013/08/16/must-read/the- mom-mystique/ (site discontinued).

# CHAPTER 3

# On Feeling Unsupported

One day, my husband and I were making our bed with freshly washed bedding. We had the sheets and the pillowcases done when someone called me, and I had to leave Jordan to finish putting the duvet cover on. Afterward, he said to me, "Gee, it's kind of tricky to get that cover on the duvet." I didn't think much of his comment until I slid into bed that night and pulled the covers over me. It was an awkward feeling. Bunched a little at the top. Not quite straight down the sides.

*Oh well,* I thought, *It will probably work its way right eventually.* It didn't. And after a few nights on a particularly tired and cranky day I thought, *THAT'S IT! I've had enough of this.* So I set to work pulling the corners of the duvet to the corners of the covers, pulling it down, pulling it to the edges, smoothing, smoothing, smoothing. And then it hit me—the thing was fundamentally flawed. My husband had put the duvet cover on the wrong way. Since our bed is king size, it's not as easy to see which edge is a length edge and which edge is a width edge. This was striking to me and made me think of how fundamentally flawed our separateness is and how, until we shift away from approaching motherhood as a disconnected work, there will always be those corners that don't quite fit.

The reason why my duvet cover didn't fit was a relatively simple discovery. The reasons why our "mothering duvet covers" aren't quite fitting may be more complicated. Regardless of the complexity involved, one factor is the erosion of family and community ties, a phenomenon which is more common in affluent societies. As it turns out, individual, community, and national wealth has the potential to be very isolating.

# When Mama Ain't Happy, Ain't Nobody Happy

The statistics on family stability support the anecdotal evidence that families are struggling in societies where extended family and community support is insufficient. Children and teenagers are having a hard time right now, and too many marriages are unwell. When extended family and community supports fall apart, is it surprising that nuclear families start falling apart too? It is possible that when extended family and community ties disappear, the burden of family nurturing and responsibility adds an extra strain on parents and marriages that are already tense. It is unreasonable to expect mothers and fathers alone to pick up what community could be contributing to our children.

From the Social Trends Institute, a research center based in New York and Barcelona, came an international report, "The Sustainable Demographic Dividend," which states:

> An abundant social-science literature, as well as common sense, supports the claim that children are more likely to flourish, and to become productive adults, when they are raised in stable, married-couple households. . . . Yet, with the global decline of these households, "the sustainability of humankind's oldest organization, the family—the fount of fertility, nurturance and human capital—is now an open question.
>
> It is not just the quantity of children that is in decline. It's the quality of their lives.[10]

This statement is further confirmed by recent publications on the family. Hillary Clinton, in her book *It Takes a Village*, discusses Cornell University psychologist Urie Bronfenbrenner's findings on the state of families in the United States.

> Bronfenbrenner has predicted for years that problems we used to think happened only to "disadvantaged" children would confront us all before long. Economic and marital instability, combined with the hectic pace and many other aspects of contemporary American

society, led him to conclude, as did other experts, that we face a silent crisis: "The present state of children and families in the United States represents the greatest domestic problem our nation has faced since the founding of the Republic. It is sapping our very roots."[11]

As the roots break down, the effects are far reaching. One example of the results of this domestic problem occurred in 1996 among a prosperous suburban county in Georgia. There was an outbreak of syphilis, affecting more than two hundred teenagers—a large portion of the teenagers were sixteen years old or younger. These kids had parties where they would do drugs and engage in group sex. Though we can't understand all of the variables, it is clear that a large factor was a lack of adult involvement. Parents would leave their teenagers alone after school until they came home after work, and with nothing else to do, the teenagers found their way to drugs, porn, and experimentation.[12]

Commenting on the STD outbreak, academic Michael Resnick, PhD, noted, "We heard a lot about emptiness. Houses that were empty and devoid of supervision, adult presence, oversight. There was for far too many of the adolescents a fundamental emptiness of purpose; a sense that they were not needed, not connected to adults, to tasks, to anything meaningful other than the raw and relentless pursuit of pleasure."[13]

When moms have strong social networks, especially if they include familial ties, that support doesn't just benefit the moms—it benefits the entire family. I see that my happiness and my ability to stay present always have an effect on my husband and my children. Like a three-legged race, we're all tied together and when one falls down, the others have a hard time staying on their feet.

# In Search of a Wonderful Life

As I have worked to build up my village, I have seen how much my children have benefited from the fellow villagers I've recruited. The book *Hold On To Your Kids* illustrates how important it is for children and adolescents to be attached to their mothers and fathers; it also convincingly explains that mothers and fathers need to create attachment villages for their children. All kids need a rich network of loving, dependable adults. The alternative to this is that children become peer centered, and the authors paint a grim picture of the damage that is done when children detach from their parents and form familial-like attachments to their peers.

When children face difficult times or struggle with challenging circumstances, the negative effects, although not erased, are diminished. by having a village of support. Grandmothers, aunts, and other trusted adults who can commit their love and time to those children can have an enormous impact on their lives, their emotional health, and their happiness. Happily, those relationships so often end up being mutually beneficial. We all need our villages back.

The potential that our extended families have to support our parenting efforts is enormous. Bruce Feiler wrote an article for the *New York Times* entitled "The Stories That Bind Us." He explained that "children who have the most self-confidence have a strong intergenerational self, they know they belong to something bigger than themselves."[14] Feiler states that a powerful way to achieve this is to share your family's stories with your children.[15] Intuitively, I could agree—I have always loved hearing family stories—even the dullest tale can be captivating to me if it reveals information about the people I came from.

After reading the article, I decided that night's dinner conversation would be a family storytelling session. My boys, who are energetic and generally find it almost unbearable to stay seated during an entire meal, were glued to their seats as they sat wide-eyed, listening to my husband and I tell our stories. We didn't have extraordinary stories to tell. There was nothing about cowboys in the Wild West or surviving a lion attack during an African safari (although there was one pretty adventurous tale of my husband being thrown into a Russian jail over a visa issue). Aside from my husband's brief imprisonment, we mostly had stories of plain moments when we ran into a bit of trouble and pulled out our courage, faith, or patience to solve our problem.

My husband began a very ordinary story about how he and his mom were driving somewhere and got lost. My youngest son was completely engrossed in the tale and with wide eyes eagerly coaxed, "What happened next!?" You could tell the outcome mattered to him. It had a simple ending. My husband explained his mom pulled over the car and said a prayer asking for help to find her way. She started driving again and was able to figure out where she was very shortly afterward.

After we shared some of our stories, our children wanted to share some of their own. One of my sons, who was four at the time, shared how sometimes, when he is at the top of a tall slide, he feels scared. When he finds himself in that situation, he just whispers to himself, "Be brave, Eliot, be brave," and then he goes for it. His courageous tale has come to my mind more than once.

That dinner was enjoyed by all of us. I don't know that my husband and I have ever been able to hold our kids' attention for so long and in such a meaningful way. I was fascinated by their keen interest and shared my experience with a friend. She recalled that she and her husband shared with their kids the story of how her husband got hit by a car in a parking lot. Their dad got hit by a car! The kids were hooked. They then told the kids, "That is why you never run or horse around in a parking lot, because you could get hit like Dad did." That was enough for them. They were convinced. She often overhears them relate their family story to their friends—they believe in parking lot safety because they have firsthand, family knowledge of what goes down in parking lots. It is almost as if it happened to them.

Not only does family history teach life lessons and connect family members but it also helps children handle stress better. Research headed by Marshall Duke, a psychologist at Emory University, supports this. Children who know their family narrative are more resilient and can deal with stress better than children who are disconnected from a larger family and their stories. The stories about the tough times and the triumphs of their predecessors help foster a child's sense of belonging to a larger family. According to the article, "a psychologist who works with children with learning disabilities, noticed [the same thing] about her students. 'The ones who know a lot about their families tend to do better when they face challenges.'"[16]

The lives and stories of our children's immediate and extended family have the potential for tremendous influence in shaping our children's choices, as well as their very crucial sense of identity. Family matters.

I think I caught the spirit of this during the summer after my daughter turned one. I had been slowly but steadily feeling more and more like my old self since that lonely visit to the doctor. The summer started off with a camping trip with my parents, an aunt, my two sisters, three of my cousins, and all of our families. I loved it. We were all in a lovely little spot, and while the children ran, explored, and played together, the adults were able to work, talk, and connect with each other. Cozy evening campfires included guitars and stories. Every night I went to sleep, I felt tired but satisfied and happy.

We were lucky to have been able to all make it. We were back from the UK, my cousin and her family were back from living in Australia, the other moved back from the States, and my sister was visiting from the other side of Canada. Although I hadn't been consistently keeping in touch with my cousins, when we came together, there was something significant in being able to introduce my children to my extended family. It made me happy to see how quickly and easily it seemed for my cousins to enjoy my children and for me to enjoy theirs. I felt like I belonged One evening, as we all gathered to pray, I felt intense gratitude that my sons could watch the entire family engage in a spiritual moment together.

After the camping trip, we all gathered once again to celebrate the baptism of my niece. Once again I basked in the camaraderie of it all and thought of *Hold On To Your Kids* and how the author states that our children grow their attachment village through us. As parents, we create that for them, and there is something so satisfying about inviting your child to attach to someone who is family. I know my niece felt loved seeing so many family members support her.

After the baptism, we traveled to Vancouver, where my husband and I stayed with my father's sister, Aunt Laura, and her husband, Uncle Ron. I strongly take after my father's side of the family, and any chance to visit with my father's family is a rare occasion, given that everyone has scattered all over.

Aunt Laura greeted me with a hug when I arrived at her home. When I looked into her eyes, I saw my father, and I also saw myself. My aunt is a strong, charismatic woman who was very involved in politics, sat on city council in Victoria, and one year she ran for mayor. Similarly interested in politics, I majored in political science in university. When I see her, I see my roots. It feels so comforting to know to whom I belong. My aunt married a man who is calm, patient, and reserved—he nicely balances her passionate and enthusiastic nature. I also married a man who is calm, patient, and reserved, and he nicely balances my passionate and enthusiastic nature.

When you share DNA with someone, their lives and their stories are particularly relevant, because the history in family often repeats itself. All of my aunts are strong, funny, resilient women, and I take courage from their lives and their triumphs; I learn from their struggles and their stumbles. Knowing them has enriched my life in a profound way.

From Vancouver, we went to my sister-in-law's wedding, where again, family abounded. It was particularly touching for me to see an elderly, hard-of-hearing grandfather, cane in hand, struggle heroically to keep up with the wedding celebrations to show his love and support for his granddaughter. I was moved by his efforts to be there, to show up for his posterity regardless of his personal discomfort.

After the wedding, we had another camp with my husband's cousins, siblings, and their children. Our kids played together in the lake and sold floats on the beach, and, again, I felt so happy that my kids could feel a part of a larger family.

After our summer travels, I arrived home tired but so grateful for family. A few days after I got home, my mom called me to let me know that her mother had died. With my oldest son, my sister, and her youngest son, I drove to Moose Jaw, Saskatchewan.

It was an exhausting nine-hour drive back to the province where I had grown up. Although Alberta and Saskatchewan are similar, there exists in some parts of Saskatchewan an almost perfect flatness. (We have a joke that in Saskatchewan, you can sit on your front porch and watch your dog run away for three days.) Some may think it a boring landscape, but in coming back it seemed to have a touch of elegance in its simplicity. We stopped to stretch our legs near a golden wheat field, and my son asked about the noisy grasshoppers. As he chased them in the ditch of the desolate gravel road we were on, I pulled out my camera and took some pictures. In trying to capture the view, I was surprised to find that I had forgotten how big the sky is there. I was brought back to the unassuming land and stretching blue skies of my youth, back to days spent in my small community, enveloped in family.

When we arrived at the funeral, I was surprised to see three of my aunts on my father's side there as well. When I mentioned my surprise, they said that of course they knew my grandmother. Of course they did. That's how those communities are. The people all know each other. I watched my mother reconnect with cousins and dear friends whom I had never met. As she spoke so familiarly with those people, I felt as if I should have known them as well.

My grandmother lived in Moose Jaw for decades and raised her children in Spring Valley, a nearby town. She was not an extraordinary woman in any way. Much like the land she lived on, my grandmother was a modest and unpretentious person whose simple life made such a stunning impact on the people around her that the large Catholic chapel where her funeral was held was brimming with her family and community.

As I was thinking about my summer awash with kinship, the image of Jimmy Stewart popped into my head. He plays the main character in *It's A Wonderful Life*. The story is of a man named George Bailey who wanted nothing more than to get out of the provincial town he grew up in and travel the world. Despite George's deep desire for adventure, he passes up opportunity after opportunity to leave, choosing family over travel. He takes over his father's business to prevent the greedy Mr. Potter from monopolizing the entire town. As George commits to a business, and then to a wife, and then to children, he finds himself tied into a life quite different from the one he had envisioned for himself. But he stays and offers himself honorably to his family and his community. When George runs into a financial crisis, putting his business and his family in jeopardy, he wonders aloud if it would have been better if he hadn't been born. An angel appears to show George how much of an impact he has made on his loved ones and shows him that because of the modest, simple, good life he lived, he truly made the world a better place.[16]

George runs home to his precious family, ready to face the difficulties he is sure lie ahead. There he discovers that the people in the community, those whom George had advocated for and helped during hard times, all showed up and donated money to help him out of his financial troubles. These weren't people he knew for a year or two or three—these were people he had grown up with, whom he'd raised his children among. They were *his* people, deeply rooted kith and kin, people who knew him and loved him. In the end, George received a hefty emotional return from his social investments; his sacrifice had brought him joy and peace.

I know I've presented a pretty rosy picture of family. I don't want to give the incorrect impression that my family is perfect, that we don't fight, or that we are all selfless, heroic souls. That's not my family. My family is full of human beings who argue and sometimes harbor bad feelings, and who don't always understand each other. We have all of that which comes, hand-in-hand, with the benefits of family. Families aren't perfect; they are often messy and complicated. But what I believe is that, in most cases, much more good than bad comes from connected families. Even if your family is kind of crazy (as most families are), it is good for kids to know where their crazy comes from. It is invaluable if your children can witness an extended family member triumph over their crazy. Knowledge is power, even in the most messed up families.

George Bailey's life, I'm sure, must seem foreign to many. In many rural communities, to stay put is seen as a sign of weakness, even failure. People leave to find jobs or to get an education, and many don't return. It is often the case that we are unable to choose where we live, as jobs take us in many different directions and sometimes across the world. This is just how life is now, but this is also one of the reasons many suffer alone and why governments can't adequately provide a system of support for people who, in earlier times, would have been supported and taken care of by extended family members.

## Sometimes Less Is More

I was running late one day to pick my son up from the bus stop, and I had to catch him at a stop farther down the line. When I arrived, there was another woman already there.

"Hi," I said. When she responded, I noticed her accent and asked where she was from. The Philippines, she answered.

I have met and loved Filipino women while visiting and living in Taiwan, Hong Kong, and Canada. They seem to have a common sense of fun, generosity, and down-to-earth humility that is always a pleasure to be around. I have heard stories of more than a few Filipino women who left their own children in the care of the grandmother to go abroad to help raise other people's children, so they could earn money for their family still living in the Philippines. Their bravery and sacrifices impress me, but my heart breaks for these women. They face tough choices.

As I was talking with the woman at the bus stop, I asked if she had any children of her own. She said she didn't have any children. Standing between heaps of snow and ice, I asked what made her decide to move to this chilly country. She told me that when she was nineteen years old, her sister—who was still in the Philippines—had been widowed and left with three small children. Her sister didn't know how she was going to support herself and her children, so this woman offered to move to Canada and work, so she could send money home to her sister and her children in the Philippines. I was blown away and told her how amazing she was. I told her that I thought that kind of familial ownership and sacrifice was much less common in Canada. She just smiled, shrugged her shoulders, and said, "Yeah, it's different here. In the Philippines, family is very important."

It seems that the more affluent a country is, the less likely that familial and community bonds can be relied on for real support.

Suniya S. Luthar, professor of Clinical and Developmental Psychology at Columbia University's Teachers College, wrote an academic article entitled "The Culture of Affluence: Psychological Costs of Material Wealth." Luthar explains that affluence can contribute to feelings of isolation and loneliness, which often lead to depression. She writes that communities bound by mutual need and discernible dependence have a greater chance for happiness, because individuals are able to show their concern and commitment toward each other by lending a hand, showing up, and sacrificing for one another. This kind of cooperation and interdependence offers opportunities for friendships and loyalties to deepen. It also gives people the chance to feel truly needed and valued by their community.

In contrast, affluent societies often "erode social capital,"[1] because instead of a good friend being a listening ear, we hire therapists; instead of family and community looking after our elderly, we pay nursing homes to take care of them; and instead of family and community raising our young, we turn to day cares. The market has largely replaced reciprocal social relationships, even though social relationships have the potential to be more emotionally satisfying.[2] Luthar explains:

> Evolutionary psychologists have suggested . . . that wealthy communities can, paradoxically, be among those most likely to engender feelings of friendlessness and isolation in their inhabitants.[3]

I have seen how, when resources are limited, we are drawn closer to our community. Once, when I was heavily pregnant, my husband went out of town for a week. In the middle of that week, I discovered, to my horror, that there was a major water leak in our back yard. The water had leaked from my yard into my basement and part of my carpet was drenched. We had just had a pricey run-in with a plumber not long before, and I knew we didn't have the money to pay another big bill. So I called my neighbor. He dropped what he was doing, came over, and fixed the water leak. Then his wife rented a carpet steam cleaner and went to work on my soggy basement carpet.

At a time when I couldn't even touch my own toes, I felt more than just relief over a problem solved. I felt validated and cared for. If I had called a plumber, we would have been able to pay with credit and eventually pay off the bill, but calling my neighbor for help was a much richer experience than a simple business transaction. It became an opportunity to develop friendship, loyalty, and gratitude—no amount of money can ever buy you that. My neighbors' act of generosity and concern made me want to help them out whenever I could. And I did—not because I owed them, but because we had become friends.

In the words of David G. Myers, from his book *The American Paradox:*

> In essence . . . the rich are the least likely to experience the security of deep social connectedness that is routinely enjoyed by people in communities where mutual dependence is often unavoidable.

> [Americans] are twice as rich and no happier. Meanwhile, the divorce rate doubled. Teen suicide tripled. Depression rates have soared, especially among teens and young adults. I call this conjunction of material prosperity and social recession the American paradox. The more people strive for extrinsic goals such as money, the more numerous their problems and the less robust their well-being.[4]

It is important to note that these scholars do not assert that wealthy people cannot find happiness or that all poor people are fountains of happiness. Extreme poverty will also negatively affect social relationships. Also, being poor in a wealthy country can be more socially isolating than being poor in a economically depressed country, especially if that country has been able to keep a strong social fabric. It's the isolation that is often the most difficult to endure. Despite the complexities, reliable research shows that high material wealth can accrue devastating psychological costs. Sometimes less is more.

## Wisdom from the Milpa

I found an extraordinary example of a productive and socially vibrant community when I visited Mexico and went on a tour of a milpa. Simply put, a milpa is a field on which local people grow food in a shared crop system. However, the spirit and soul of a milpa is much more. Our guide explained how the people in the area in which he grew up all worked a common field and harvested together. These shared agricultural lands can be found in central-southeastern Mexico and northern Central America. This communal effort has existed for hundreds of years, a way of life for many communities that has been passed down for many generations.

The milpa merges economics and community at the same time, the goals being convergent rather than divergent. Historically, milpas have been able to yield large crops of food without the use of artificial pesticides or fertilizers and without depleting or exhausting the soil. I was intrigued to learn about a people who were not committed to "biggering and biggering and biggering"[5] as the Once-ler boasted in *The Lorax*.

Although no farmer on a milpa can claim to be rich monetarily, they appear to be rich in other important ways. They have a very vibrant family and community life. I loved hearing how much power, influence, and respect is given to the mama of the family. In talking to my guide, it was clear the role of family is taken very seriously. These communities deserve our attention, because they are inspiring models of strong family and community ties in cultures that as yet do not have the baggage many affluent cultures carry.

I am not under any illusion that life is perfect on the milpas. I'm sure there are struggles, tensions, injustices, and disadvantages. What *is* clear to me, however, is that their family and community ties are much stronger than in most affluent societies.

When I came back from Mexico, my continued interest in milpas led me to scour the Internet in search of more information. That is when I found The Milpa Project.

The Milpa Project has been organized by a group of individuals who are passionate about the benefits of this ancient way of life. In their words, "[Milpas are the] world's best examples of sustainable agriculture."[6] They worry that the beautiful and important aspects of the milpa—tradition, community, access to food sources, and sustenance for the spirit—will be lost with growing globalization and pressures of modernity. The Milpa Project website explains that "milpa crops are nutritionally and environmentally complementary. . . . The milpa, in terms of maintaining soil fertility, and providing a variety of healthy foods, and limiting environmental impacts of food production, may well be one of the most successful human inventions ever developed."[7]

As my curiosity about milpas grew, I found a particularly interesting story about the value of milpas from Berkley graduate Linda Green. Green is currently an associate professor of anthropology and director of Latin studies at Arizona University. She spent two years in Guatemala as an anthropologist with a Mayan community. Interviewing local widows, she found that because of the violence of the government against the Mayan people at that time, many women were left without husbands to help work on their milpas and take care of their families. One widow asked Green if she would help her buy 200–300 pounds of fertilizer for her twenty-by-twenty-foot piece of land, which she was depending on for sustenance for her and her three children. When Green lent a hand, other widows in the area asked for help as well and exchanged handiwork, small carvings, or fruit in exchange for the fertilizer.

Green decided to work out the actual cost of growing the corn versus buying it at the local market. Surprisingly, she found that it actually was more cost effective to simply buy the corn rather than grow it on the milpa. When she explained this to the women, they told her that giving up the milpa was giving up more than just homegrown corn.

As Green spent time with the Mayan women, she heard them talk reverently about corn and its importance in Mayan diet, culture, and community. One of the women, Margarita, explained to Green all the practical advantages that the milpa-grown corn provided. The corn not only offers sustenance but the stalks also act as building material and food sweetener. The cobs feed the people's animals. Husks are useful in cooking and have medicinal uses as well. "The milpa is more than just corn," Margarita stated, "the milpa is an entire world, a way of life."[8]

The milpa is also a place where the people believe their ancestors reside. Many Mayas believe that family ties extend beyond this life and that the spirits of parents and grandparents return to the milpa to watch over their posterity. One elder explained that working in the milpa actually evoked the presence of his ancestors. For many Mayas who work the milpa, "working the soil reconnects them with the dead, Mother Earth, and the spirits of the mountains, volcanoes, rivers, and trees."[9]

People see the milpa as a way of protecting their future as well as their past. Children are taught how to grow, prepare, and eat corn. Young girls learn corn preparation from their mothers and boys learn the work of their fathers on the milpa. Before planting, the boys are taught the prayers that are recited to the ancestors and spirits.

I spoke with The Milpa Project's project manager, Brenda Armstrong, a British Columbia Canadian who divides her time between her homeland and San Felipe in Baja California, Mexico. She mentioned that although the people of the milpa are grappling with competing interests of the modern economy of San Felipe, the people in the area have not been pushed to abandon the culture of family, because extended family members continue to support each other.

Brenda spoke about how often there are aunts and grandmothers with many children playing around their homes because their mothers need to work, sell their tortillas, or otherwise engage in the local economy. There seems to be an abundance of willing relatives, often living in close proximity, who can watch the little ones. Childcare is observed to be a fluid offering, without the expectation of monetary payment between family members. Brenda also mentioned that during her travels throughout Mexico, she's noticed an exceptional amount of support that mothers receive from other female relatives. This setup that Brenda described—having grandmothers and aunties being such a big part of children's everyday lives—would be something that I know my children would love so much. I would love it, too.

Mexico is not the only place where this is the case. While waiting in line at the checkout counter here in Canada, I struck up a conversation with an older African lady. I learned that she looked after her grandson while her daughter worked. I remarked how generous that was of her, and she replied how shocked she was that many grandparents in Canada don't feel a sense of responsibility toward their grandchildren. In her culture, grandparents are expected to contribute to the well-being of the grandchildren. At the same time, as the grandparents' age, they are not dumped off in a lonely nursing home. Instead, they are surrounded by the family they loved and supported their entire lives.

This is not the kind of society I was raised in or that I have brought my children into. Having been born in an affluent country, it has fallen into my lap to reinvent a familial-type village for myself and my family. Ideally, there should be an established community of women who are familiar enough to know when and how to help each other. Instead, community building is another item of business on many mothers' to-do lists. It is a stretch for many who are already stretched too thin.

But not having such a familial-type village forces us to rely on less socially and emotionally satisfying alternatives. A government solution, hired hand, or even group of friends, no matter how fantastic they are, could never in reality replace what family has to offer, especially when children enter the scene. As close as we may feel to our beloved friends, there is something eternally magnetic about family ties.

I know a lot of people think that staying with their family would be hard—even unhealthy—and that they are better off far away from them. In some family situations, this may be the case. However, when people are stuck with family, like it or not, they learn how to coexist, even though it may take many people decades to learn how to do so peaceably. It's possible that many of us have lost the art of getting along. We make our visits once a year, find them difficult and exhausting, and are glad that we can leave those complex relationships behind. But perhaps it is because we leave that conflicts stay unresolved, frustrating, and complex. Because we don't live close together, we don't have to set up firm boundaries and take important stands and forgive and love and work together and slowly build a lifetime of support and history mingled with difficulty. I am saying this as a natural runner—I love to run away from difficult or uncomfortable situations. So, yes, I am writing about myself; however, I can't help but see that we as a society are missing out on the major benefits of this safety net, this familial tapestry.

And so we find ourselves, tugging at corners that will never fit and smoothing edges that will never be smooth. The glimmer of hope here is that once I realized that my duvet cover was on the wrong way, I was able to turn the cover around. Once I faced my annoyance and sought to understand my problem, I found the snug corners and smooth edges that I wanted. Facing and understanding a problem is an important part of finding a solution. When we can see clearly how and why we are missing our villages, the next step is to look to different examples of village living to figure out what kind of village we want to build for ourselves.

# ENDNOTES

1.  Suniya S. Luthar, "The Culture of Affluence: Psychological Costs of Material Wealth," *Child Development* 74, no. 6 (2003): 1581–1593.

2.  Ibid.

3.  Ibid.

4.  David G. Myers, *The American Paradox: Spiritual Hunger in an Age of Plenty* (New Haven, CT: Yale University Press, 2000).

5.  Dr. Seuss, *The Lorax* (New York: Random House, 1971).

6.  The Milpa Project. http://www.themilpaproject.com/the_team.html.

7.  Ibid.

8.  Linda Green, *Fear as a Way of Life: Mayan Widows in Rural Guatemala* (New York: Columbia University Press, 1999).

9.  Ibid.

10. "What Do Marriage and Fertility Have to Do with the Economy?" *The Sustainable Demographic Dividend* (Charlottesville: University of Virginia, 2012), http://sustaindemographicdividend.org/wp-content/uploads/2012/07/SDD-2011-Final.pdf.

11. Hillary Rodham Clinton, *It Takes a Village* (New York: Simon & Schuster, 2006), 314.

12.  Rachel Dretzin, "The Lost Children of Rockdale County," *Frontline*, directed by Rachel Dretzin and Barak Goodman, aired October 19, 1999 (Arlington, VA: PBS, 1999).

13. Michael D. Resnick, PhD, "Adrift in America," PBS, http://www.pbs.org/wgbh/pages/frontline/shows/georgia/isolated/resnick.html.

14. 14. Bruce Feiler, "The Stories That Bind Us," *New York Times*, March 15, 2013, http://www.nytimes.com/2013/03/17/fashion/the-family-stories-that-bind-us-this-life.html?_r=0.

15. Ibid.

16. Frances Goodrich et al., *It's A Wonderful Life*, Directed by Frank Capra (Liberty Films, 1947).

# CHAPTER 4

# Attachment Villages

When I went to the Canadian Museum of History in Ottawa, I saw an exhibit there on the matrilineal Iroquois Native American who lived together as extended families in longhouses. I was mesmerized by it. I went through this exhibit six months after I had Sadie, a time when I was feeling particularly tired, lonely, and challenged as a mother. When I read the accounts of the Iroquois life, I felt jealous of the women and, in that moment, longed for what they had.

Longhouses were large enough to hold a hundred or more people. They were framed with poles that were covered with large sheets of bark, attached with lashing. They were places that hosted neighborly visits, storytelling, and political discussion.

Inside, families were sectioned off with a row of hearths running down the center of the longhouse between the family compartments. Families shared those hearths and used them for light, warmth, and cooking. The practical necessity of warmth and a place for cooking provided a gathering place for families—a place to exchange news, recount ancient stories, and discuss the matters of the day. The hearths brought to mind my own experiences of open-hearted talks around cozy campfires, and my envy deepened.

Being a matrilineal people, when women married, they were not separated from their mother and sisters; all in-laws would come to live with the matrilineal line, including the grandmother and great aunts. The older women held authority within the longhouse, the oldest being the clan mother who held great social and political influence. Clan mothers appointed the community chiefs and made changes to their appointments as they saw fit. They were always consulted by the chiefs on matters of war and peace negotiations.

Similar to the farmers of the milpas, the people of a longhouse worked a common field and the harvest was divided equally among them. Unlike patriarchal cultures, in the Iroquois matriarchal society, the matriarch of the family had legitimate control over the fields while the men worked them. The women stayed busy near the longhouse with all the children as they prepared food and made clothing, mats, and dolls. They also excelled at making beautiful clay pots, using techniques handed down from the accumulated expertise of the generations of women who came before them.

After walking through the exhibit, I fantasized about what living like that would feel like. Mothering in an intimate way, like the Iroquois, would assuredly have its drawbacks, but it would definitely have its advantages. Children would keep each other company while mothers would be able to both be with them and work at skilled tasks, such as the crafts of pottery and other artwork. You also wouldn't have to feel any guilt about not being a fun mom or an organized mom or a creative mom or an informed mom, because you *wouldn't have to be everything.* That's one of the benefits of working together; you offer the best you have and benefit from the best of others.

Women enjoy the various stages of childhood differently. Some women are amazing with teenagers, others are magic with toddlers, and still others are baby whisperers. Ideally, mothers would combine their strengths and natural gifts and share them with all the children. This would allow the children to benefit from a variety of strengths and abilities. Perhaps in this setting kids really could "have it all."

If you suffered from postpartum depression, maybe the other women would just keep an eye on your other little ones while you rested and slept and got better. Or if you struggled with a disability, your sisters would be right there to help you every day until the end of it all. If you had an autistic child or one with a disability or difficulty, you wouldn't have to bear the burden all by yourself. As I have waded deeper into life with kids, I have come to see that the ideal for my husband and me, as well as the other parents we know, would be an integrated, committed, and loving network of grandparents, aunts, and uncles who live in close proximity. It could be a superior way to meet our children's (and our own) needs.

Raising children in a communal way would benefit the older generation as well as the younger. Instead of placing our grandmothers and grandfathers in assisted living homes and nursing homes, lonely and craving family, they could live in the longhouse, readily available to cuddle a baby while its mother was busy. Perhaps those aching arms are aching for a reason; they were meant to be used, not shelved because of an assumed expiration date. And the burden of caring for the older grandparents would be shared among all the women.

We see gaps in our mothering efforts and feel like these gaps should not be there. However, it is ridiculous and wrong to think that the solution is to keep dumping more and more guilt on ourselves to spur us to work harder, to be more okay with being miserable, and to just get by, anxious and exhausted, with a feeling of failure shadowing our days. One woman was never meant to replace an entire village.

As Linda Napikoski, a women's history expert, wrote:

> Communal living . . . is often recalled as a hippie ideal and is usually not taken seriously as a viable alternative to the nuclear family. However, the so-called traditional family, with a household consisting of only two parents and their children, is actually a relatively new concept in human history. It was more a reflection of and benefit to the industrial revolution than a historically necessary system.[1]

Although communal living is, historically, a more common lifestyle, it would be a tough sell to try to get my parents and my sisters to leave their houses and move into a longhouse with me. My husband probably wouldn't go for it either. Admittedly, I was dreaming of the Iroquois through rose-colored glasses. I have no way of knowing how those women actually felt about their lives. What *was* clear to me in that museum was that my mothering experience could look radically different from what it was looking like at that time. It was the start of my search for examples of people and cultures who mother in completely different ways than I was.

# Taking Notes from Mothers Around the World

I wanted to find out more about cultures like the Iroquois and the people on milpas, cultures that excel at supporting mothers and their families by making community a priority. I found some compelling and inspiring examples from the past and from around the world.

When looking at examples of mothering from the past, I wanted to look back, not just hundreds, but thousands, of years. When I found what I was looking for, I felt tremendously comforted as I read of how early women cooperatively approached their work as mothers. Although I turned to many sources in my interest-driven research, I found the work of Sarah Hrdy to be the most illuminating. Sarah Hrdy, PhD, from Harvard, is a member of the National Academy of Sciences and Professor Emerita of Anthropology at the University of California-Davis. In her groundbreaking book entitled *Mothers and Others,* Hrdy offers amazing insight into our mothering heritage, looking as far back as the early humans.

She explains that for decades, anthropologists have looked to apes to gather information about how early humans raised their young. However, one overlooked, but important, difference that Hrdy shares is that both male and female apes, unlike most humans, are often violent to related offspring, seeing them as potential competition for resources. For this reason, among others she documents, ape mothers rarely practice shared care of their infants.

Hrdy rejects comparing our parenting ideal with that of apes as she offers strong evidence that human beings would not have been able to flourish as they have without practicing shared care when raising their children. Hrdy instead champions the key role of *allomothers*—females who are not the biological mother of a child but who play a role in the mothering and upbringing of that child. The story of humankind wouldn't be the same without the help of allomothers.

I was entranced as I read Hrdy's work. Her words, though academic, felt magical to me. My heart warmed as I read her extraordinary account of the impact mothers, grandmothers, aunties, and young girls have had on the history and survival of humankind. Her research also lent color and legitimacy to something that I, along with most mothers, feel intuitively. We, along with most of the mothers who came before us for most of history, have understood that it takes a village to raise a child.

As previously mentioned in chapter one, in cultures where mothers are supported by a community of women, the incidences of postpartum depression are significantly decreased. Cultures where female relatives take care of the mother during the postpartum period, perform personal care rituals (which are practiced by many women in Guatemala, Mayan women in the Yucatan, and Latina women both in the United States and Mexico), prescribe mandated rest (found among new Punjabi mothers), give functional assistance (having other women take care of older children and other duties the new mother usually performs), and provide social recognition of the new mother's new role and status yield mentally healthier postpartum periods for new mothers.[2] In turn, the mother who is taken care of later assists in taking care of the other new mothers in her family.

Another example comes from the Japanese Gotō Islands, where pediatrician Dr. T. Berry Brazelton found that new mothers were sent to their mothers' homes with their babies and rested there for a month. "Their only job was to feed their babies,"[3] as female relatives took care of the new mother.

Hrdy also wrote about several traditional foraging cultures that exist today, including the Hadza, !Kung, Aka, Efe, and Mbuti. Hrdy mentions that Yanomamö and Himba allomothers physically bond with young ones. In the majority cultures in the Human Relations Area Files, before the natural mother's milk comes in, the other women will take turns breastfeeding babies who are not their own. Among some groups, as the baby grows, allomothers will chew food in their mouths and pass it from their mouths to the child's through "kiss feeding." Though this may seem an unappealing way to bond with babies, the underlying sentiment is helpful—physical and emotional closeness facilitates bonding people to babies who are not biologically theirs.[4] It seems that in many of these cultures, the allomothers develop strong bonds to the children who they will help to raise, starting in the children's infancies—a difficult task for many women in developed societies who, for various reasons, are unable to remain close to a larger extended family.

In all of the cultures Hrdy writes about, the mothers present their babies to the group and, in many instances, encourage the other adults and children to cuddle, kiss, nurse, sing to, and talk to their new babies.

> [They] understand how beneficial it is for a baby to be introduced to a community of others. By sharing her baby, the mother sends a clear signal that both she and her offspring will be counting on help from the clan. By exposing alloparents to the sight, sound, and smell of her alluring little charge, the mother lays the groundwork for emotional ties binding her baby to potential caretakers and vice versa.[5]

According to Hrdy, wherever people live in traditional ways, rather than "compartmentalized families . . . shared care is the rule."[6] This is the case for the Aka in Central Africa, the Agta in the Philippines, the Onge foragers on the Andaman Islands off the eastern coast of India, the Trobriand Islanders in the Pacific, and more.

As our society has moved away from cooperative mothering among extended family units and into communities where we may know our neighbors only superficially, our natural instincts of distrust have put us in a position similar to the apes'. When mothers don't feel totally confident about the available allomothers, they often will end up mothering alone, which is a more taxing, less efficient, and unnatural way for humans to raise children.

On the central Caroline Islands in the Pacific Ocean, within the Federated States of Micronesia, live the Ifaluk people. According to Betzig, Harrigan, and Turke:

> Ifaluk mothers live on average with roughly four other adult women on their matrilineal estates, they spend only about half of their day time associating with their own children, and only about half of that time alone with them, they may actually spend more time alone with older than with younger children. Alloparents, especially close, female, elder kin, spend a lot of time with young children, and having living mothers, sisters, and daughters may have a positive effect on the number of children women produce. These results

are consistent with accumulating evidence that extended family co-residence [and] cooperative childcare . . . are all more common in traditional cultures than in ours.[7]

Extended family co-residence is also the norm in Pakistan. I met and spoke with two Pakistani women in the park one day. While our children played, I asked them how their mothering experience here in Canada compared to their experience back in Pakistan. One of the women said that in Pakistan, extended families often live in what she called "joint families." She explained:

> In joint families, you don't just think about yourself; you think about mother, father, brothers, sisters, everybody. There are many problems living this way, but there are also many good things as well—for our kids especially. They grow up with their grandma, grandpa, cousins. They learn the importance of relatives. They also learn compromise, how to work together with others, and how to handle differences. Whenever you have a problem, you never think, "I am alone." Everybody shares your problem—the others care about you and take care of you.

While not diminishing the challenges many Pakistani women face, the potential for access to a variety of allomothers in their joint families offers advantages that many mothers in more industrialized countries only dream of. The two Pakistani mothers I spoke with both agreed that raising children in Canada was a lonelier, more isolated experience than in Pakistan. Even in speaking with my doctor, who was born in Pakistan and whose family still lives there, I learned that her family had purchased a large housing complex comprised of several apartments where her extended family lives. She explained, "In Pakistan, everything revolves around the mom. Family is very important."

Although many of these cultures seem to have less in some ways, their social organization is superior when compared with many affluent countries. This is especially true of children's access to an extended network of support, which can be very important (especially to children who are at risk). According to Hrdy:

> Historians of the family like Stephanie Coontz, along with anthropologists, psychologists, and social workers, have long been aware

that, across time and in diverse locales, infants born into poverty, at low birth weight or premature, or to a teenage or unmarried mother tend to do better cognitively, emotionally, and physically if they grow up in extended families. . . . A vast cross-disciplinary literature attests to the fact that mothers with more social support are more responsive to their infants' needs. . . . As Coontz puts it, "Children do best in societies where childrearing is considered too important to be left entirely to parents."[8]

I have seen in my own life how having other adults nurture me as a child was extremely important. During my years of junior high and high school, I had a fun, wise, and caring allomother who wove me into her life and helped me through some tough teenage years. She was family to me, and she played a part in shaping who I am today.

While this is perhaps an obvious point, it's essential to remember that children who have a few engaged, committed adults in their lives—people who show up for them and who they know they can count on—show stronger mental, social, and emotional development than those who do not. According to researchers van IJzendoorn, Sagi, and Lambermon, "the most powerful predictor of later socioemotional development involves the quality of the entire attachment network."[9] In fact, researchers Kermoian and Leiderman found that among the Gusii villagers in Kenya, the babies who were securely attached to their multiple caretakers showed better mental development than those who were weakly or anxiously attached.[10]

The spirit of our mothering heritage, the communal way mothers have mothered for thousands of years and continue to mother in some parts of the world today, is something that I hope we mothers can appreciate in our hearts and perhaps be instructed by as we consider the quality of our own mothering communities.

## Closer to Home

So what if you don't live on a Japanese archipelago or in the Caroline Islands with the Ifaluk people? I hope that the stories of mothers I've shared can serve to inform the choices we make as mothers about our own networks of support. Although I find the examples I've just shared to be inspiring, I'd like to also offer some less exotic examples of supported mothers—examples that we might more easily implement into our own communities. The first is from a mother of six, now a grandmother to nine, who started her mothering career in Canada in the 1970s.

> Times were different then. We were living in a complex where there were a lot of stay-at-home moms. I was only there for a couple of years, but we had a real web of support, because we all lived so close and because there were so many of us. We were always there for each other because of those two factors. We shared babysitting all the time, so much so that we had a babysitting co-op. The way it worked was you signed up and then received points when you babysat other children, and then when it came time for you to have someone else babysit your children, you would call someone up in the co-op and ask, "Hey, are you available at such-and-such a time for my three kids?" And if they babysat your kids, you would give them your points. We would take turns being the person monitoring the points.

> It was great because the kids got to spend time at different people's houses and got to know different people. Also, it was just easy because you didn't have to worry, "Oh, how can I return this favor?" If someone ran late, it wasn't a big deal, because you knew you were getting more points.

> There was also a nice feeling of camaraderie that came with being a part of this group of women who were all doing the same thing and who were all living so closely together in that complex. I've never seen anything like that since.

> When I had five children, we moved into the Belgravia neighborhood in Edmonton, and I loved mothering there as well, because there were many stay-at-home moms. My next-door neighbor and I became good friends, and our kids were always back and forth between our homes. I also became close with two families who lived across the street. One of the families, the Ungers, had a son, Peter, who was the same age as one of our sons. He had two older sisters

who had already left home so he was kind of on his own. He was over at our house all the time—we even had a job chart for him. He is still close to our family. We have an incredible bond of friendship that will never be broken with the whole Unger family because of Peter. As a grandmother now, I have a long-range perspective; I can see the result of things that happened when I was a young mother.

Another way we developed close friendships with other families was spending time on vacations together. We would read to our children together and cook together and our children would play in the water and sit around the campfire together. All of those kids are all grown up now, but they are very much connected to each other; there's still a real bond there.

It's really important for kids in the teenage and young adult years to know that there are other adults who care for them. It makes a difference for them in how they feel connected to the whole world. It's important for them to know that there are people other than their parents who know them and trust and have faith in them.

My youngest daughter, Rachel, had a close group of friends in high school who always liked to go to each other's houses. They spent their free time at each other's houses on the weekends and after school. They were all really busy girls with cross-country and music and volunteering, but during their down time, they were welcome in any of the homes. The moms were there offering food and a place to relax. This is an important thing for teenagers to have—a place to go and food to share. All of the moms took an interest in the girls and would talk with them, and pretty soon the moms started to connect with each other and we became a sort of mother-daughter group. Not that we got together a lot, but we felt really connected because our daughters were so connected. They all participated in Rachel's wedding, and we still get together once or twice a year even though it's been almost six years since all the girls graduated. The girls know that they are really loved by all these moms who they grew up with. And that's really special—when you are connected through your children to another parent, there's a very strong bond that develops. It's almost like family, because you have these other parents who love your children.

At the same time Rachel was enjoying her group of friends, my son, David, who is a few years older than Rachel, had found a similar group. He had a small group of friends who loved to come over to our house. It's important for kids to connect in homes rather than just public places. It's safer. One day, my husband and I had left the house and then came home to find David's friends in our house. They knew the security code and knew how to get in, so they just let themselves in. It was really fun for them, they were just like, "Hey, hi!" I was glad that they felt so at home with us and that our home was a place they wanted to be at. Those guys all had a lot of fun together and knew that they were welcome and cared for in each other's homes. Whenever you can get that going, it's remarkable to experience.

—Coleen

Although this account is of a woman who was a stay-at-home mom at a time when many moms stayed at home, I think it is still valuable for stay-at-home and working moms today as well. Coleen's mother-daughter group included working mothers as well as stay-at-home moms. The essence of her experience was that their family was deliberate in their efforts to spend time forging bonds with other families who were committed to working toward the same thing. They prioritized having an open-door policy in their home and made an effort to welcome their kids' friends into their space and their lives.

Another great example of a group of neighbors who adopted each other's children is the following story from a Utah mom:

I had such a great experience living in what we called "the cul-de-sac," where my son felt all too comfortable knocking on our neighbor's door and asking if they had anything good to eat. He would go to our neighbor, who was a nurse, to remove slivers. In winters, there was always a huge fort constructed for snow play, and the kids and grownups stayed out late on summer nights playing baseball in the cul-de-sac. One year for Christmas, most of the kids got hockey sticks, and street hockey was the new favorite activity. We shared garden veggies and planned little holiday parties. The kids all knew that any mom would help them, love them, and, when needed, discipline them. We even had moms' night out at the movies (right down the street at the neighbor's house on the big screen TV). Many of my best memories come from this special place where we all felt community and you could always knock on your neighbor's door for that cup of sugar.

There was a time when I felt like my culture was too fragmented to facilitate the togetherness that mothers really need. For a long time, there was no part two in this book. I personally know how easy it is to get discouraged. But although mothers have a rich history of togetherness, mothers have also had a history of having to rebuild their social networks after wars, diseases, natural disasters, and social changes. Saying good-bye has always been a part of life. The struggle to find love and connection with others is an ancient theme of humankind. In our modern day, our challenges are unique, but I think they are not impossible to maneuver if we are willing to make some changes and reconsider our priorities. In part two, I offer some tools that mothers can use to build their own bustling, vibrant, and beautiful villages.

# ENDNOTES

1.  Linda Napikoski, "Collective Mothering: Does It Take a Mother to Raise a Child?" AboutEducation, accessed March 10, 2015, http://womenshistory. about.com/od/feministtexts/a/collective_mothering.htm.

2.  Kathleen Kendall-Tackett, PhD, IBCLC, *How Other Cultures Prevent Postpartum Depression: Social Structures that Protect New Mothers' Mental Health*, Uppity Science Chick, accessed March 10, 2015, http://www.uppitysciencechick. com/how_other_cultures.pdf.

3.  T. Berry Brazelton, PhD, *Learning to Listen: A Life Caring for Children* (Boston: Da Capo Press, 2013).

4.  Sarah Hrdy, PhD, *Mothers and Others: The Evolutionary Origins of Mutual Understanding* (Cambridge: Harvard University Press, 2011), 76.

5.  Ibid., 78–79.

6.  Ibid.

7.  Laura L. Betzig, Alisa Harrigan, and Paul Turke, "Childcare on Ifaluk," *Zeitschrift für Ethnologie*, 114 (1989): 17, 161–177, http://www.jstor.org/ stable/25842108.

8.  Hrdy, *Mothers and Others*, 131.

9.  Marinus van IJzendoorn, Abraham Sagi, and Mirjam W. E. Lambermon, "The Multiple Caretaker Paradox: Data from Holland and Israel," in *Beyond the Parents: The Role of Other Adults in Children's Lives*, ed. R. C. Pianta (San Francisco: Jossey-Bass, 1992), 5–24.

10. Rosanne Kermoian and P. Herbert Leiderman, "Infant Attachment to Mother and Child Caretaker in an East African Community," *International Journal of Behavioral Development* 9 (1986): 455–469.

# Part II

# Where Do We Go From Here?

The most important thing to get for your baby is not a Rock 'n Play, nor a good set of swaddling blankets, nor a high-end stroller. *The most important thing to get for your baby is a village.* Your village will keep you afloat. It will carry you when you are tired, feed you when you are starving, forgive you when you are unkempt and hours late. They will love your baby when you are too tired or frustrated to hold her at the moment, because you are imperfect and human and have imperfect and human failings. They will remind you who you are when you start to think your whole life is only about poop. They will lift you up.

—Karyn Thurston, author of the blog Girl of Cardigan

O ur need for attachment villages has not diminished just because the villages have. In attempting collective mothering, you may not have much luck trying to recruit a bunch of your friends and family to sell their homes and go live on a commune, but there are ways to start building attachment villages in our modern, transient, often disconnected societies.

In Part II, I discuss changes we can make in how we think, how we act, and how we organize ourselves that can help us move toward a more connected and supported mothering experience. The ideas in the following chapters have been developed through feedback from other moms, research, and personal experience. They include appreciating our interdependence, embracing our strengths as women, seeking out and creating places to connect, developing our inner mystics, embracing diversity, accepting help, strengthening our emotional health, serving our fellow moms, and weaving our hearts and lives together.

These suggestions are meant to be helpful for full-time stay-at-home moms, part-time working moms, and full-time working moms. These are not three different groups of women; rather, most women, at various points in their lives, have probably fulfilled all three roles. The strategies a stay-at-home mom uses may be different than strategies used by a mom who works full- or part-time.

A friend of mine who is a mother of two young girls and a partner at a law firm shared this with me:

> It's different for working moms than it is for stay-at-home moms. I . . . work all day, alongside other intelligent, interesting women. So, I'm not alone in the same way. The weird thing for me is that a switch flips when I leave "work" and put my "mom" hat on. The isolation is more short-lived (evenings and weekends) but it's also more acute since I really don't have any "mom" connections the way many SAHMs [stay-at-home moms] do—the people I spend my day with are not the same people I parent around at night.
>
> Given my limited time with my kids, I don't make a lot of those parent connections since I'm really focused on what my kids are up to. As a result, I find myself feeling very alone at school concerts and soccer games where other parents seem to know each other (or my nanny) but not me.

In contrast, another friend of mine has been a stay-at-home mom for thirteen years and has lived in the same neighborhood for over fifteen years. As she invested years living in the same neighborhood and had a relatively flexible workday with children at home, it was easier for her to make connections with the people of her community and to get to know the moms whose children hang out with or go to school with her own children. Now she can't go to the local grocery store without running into someone she knows. She tells her older children, "You better watch yourselves when you're out and about, because I have eyes *all* over the neighborhood." This has enabled her to foster connection in a different way and also left her looking for a different kind of connection than the lawyer in my previous example. During her days at home, she hasn't had the same built-in access to the camaraderie that can come with coworkers and the satisfaction of working with an adult team who values, depends on, and shows appreciation for her efforts and contributions as do many women who work outside the home.

My hope is that, regardless of your situation, you will be able to take the ideas I offer and tailor them to your own unique circumstance. Your solutions won't look the same as those of the woman next to you, but, hopefully, this part of the book will inspire you to discover some powerful connections that help strengthen you and your family.

# CHAPTER 5

# Declaring Our Interdependence

*For centuries we have declared our independence. Perhaps it's now time that we as humans declare our interdependence.*
—Tiffany Schlain

When I had my children, I knew that they were a part of me and that our happiness was, and would be forever, connected—we are one. A mother sees close up the reality of the condition of humanity; our happinesses are all connected. I don't stop where you begin. This is a holy mountaintop mothers are privileged to be brought to. Although we intuitively understand this truth with regard to our children, it is sometimes easy to forget our interconnectedness with others around us.

Charlie Todd, in a TED talk entitled "The Shared Experience of Absurdity," describes his decision to take improv everywhere. He launched his own improv project in 2002 called Improv Everywhere. Todd explains, "One of the points of Improv Everywhere is to cause a scene in a public place that is a positive experience for other people. It's a prank, but it's also a great story to tell."[1] He recounts one of his projects that took place on a cold January day. Todd organized seven men to board a New York subway train, each from a different stop, wearing everything except a pair of pants. The men walked on leisurely and acted as if they didn't know each other. He hid a video camera, which caught one woman's reaction as the first man boarded. She looked surprised and seemed to be a little nervous when the second man without pants boarded. She didn't crack a smile until she made eye contact with two Danish men sitting across from her who were laughing, and then she broke into a huge smile, covering her face to hide her laughter.

In the TED talk, after showing the moment in the video where the girl smiles, Charlie Todd states, "I love that moment in the video. Before it became a shared experience, it was something that was a little bit scary or at least something that was confusing to her, and then once it became a shared experience, it was funny and something that she could laugh at."[2]

The most fulfilled life is one where our shared experiences become so numerous that we find ourselves living shared existences. And this power and importance of a shared existence is not limited to people. The smallest units of matter here on earth and throughout the universe are not stand-alone heroes either. An atom is a family of protons, neutrons, and electrons. Protons must be different from neutrons, and electrons must be different than protons and neutrons. It is, in fact, their very differences that bring them together. Atoms, the essential building blocks of life, would be a sea of nothingness if they lived isolated and separate existences. They become something substantial only when they combine with other atoms and create molecules. It is, again, only when molecules such as proteins, lipids, carbo-hydrates, and nucleic acid come together, join hands, and sing the song of molecular love that they are able to form cells. The little humble cell, in a comfortable niche of like-minded cells, performs the same tasks that your body as a whole performs.

Every little cell in your entire body looks for breakfast in the morning—just like you. It digests its food, converts energy, and excretes waste—just like you do. It breathes in and out and reproduces when the time is right. The cell is like a little mini organism.

We as people are also units, the building blocks of the whole of humanity on this planet. We, like atoms, are also interconnected, whether we want to be or not. People connect and come together to form family units. Family units come together to form communities, which are the building blocks of towns and cities. Towns and cities are connected to form provinces or states, which form countries. And countries, like organs, all have an effect on each other.

Our world is at a unique place in history, where business and economic interests have never been more interconnected. We are like the cells of this world, and what we do as individuals, the world does as a whole. When individuals are cruel and selfish, the world becomes cruel and selfish; when individuals are peaceful and loving, the world becomes peaceful and loving. What happens at a micro level transcends to the macro. All of our private choices have public consequences, because we are deeply interconnected. The developing philosophy of *prioritizing* individualism and independence is a short-sighted and dangerous direction.

The following from thebrainbank.scienceblog.com explains what happens when cells ignore the good of the whole for the sake of their own agendas in a post entitled, "Cancer, When Good Cells Go Bad":

> Most cells in our body behave the way they should. When they get signals from the tissue surrounding them telling them to multiply, they will divide into two new cells; when they get old or damaged they will kill themselves in a cell-suicide process called apoptosis. Cells are very altruistic in this way; they even have the good grace to package all their remnants into little membrane-bound sacks that other cells can come along and chow down on. Cancer cells are not altruistic. While normal cells function solely to benefit the organism as a whole, cancer cells have their own agenda and that is to stay alive and to keep dividing. The problem for our body is that when a cancer cell goes forth and multiplies uncontrollably, a mass of cells form and that mass is a tumour. . . . Cancer cells show the ability to adapt and thrive as individual cells at the expense of the body as a whole.[3]

Although those cancer cells are gratifying their immediate desire to stay alive, by killing off their host, they are inevitably headed toward their own end. While the healthy cells do what they can for the body as a whole and for the next generation of cells, cancer cells bring doom and death for themselves as well as the next generation. Cancer cells are motivated by self-interest and self-preservation. However, "the survival of a multi-celled organism relies on teamwork. Working together, specialized cells carry out life functions, such as digestion, breathing, and circulation. Such organization is key to developing complex life forms," as well as for whole communities.[4]

While I was thinking about how there are similarities to be found between cells, people, and the global population, I stumbled upon this lovely bit of prose from a Facebook page called "Fractalism."

> It always sort of calms me to know that the most basic patterns in nature, and in the universe, are found in every scale of life and matter that humans know. I find comfort in knowing that whenever something comes from a point of origin, it will take on a specific pattern. That trees, look like blood vessels, look like the branches of your lungs, look like river bed's flowing off of the great mighty mountains, look like the roots that grow into the earth to absorb nutrients, look like the veins of a leaf. That waves on the mighty ocean look like sound waves, look like ripples in one's consciousness, look like waves of light, look like the aftermath of the impact of a gigantic bomb. And that the mitosis of the smallest cell resembles the most immense supernova of the biggest red dwarf star in a distant galaxy. Every pattern in nature repeats itself, in an infinity of ways, in a scale both up, and down.[5]

What is true up, down, sideways, and backward is that we mothers can take a lesson from the tiny atom that knows and lives this truth: alone it is nothing, but united with others, it is the whole world, the universe, and beyond. As the Sufi poet Rumi said, "You are not a drop in the ocean—you are the entire ocean in a drop."

Being the entire ocean in a tiny drop places us in a state that is more easily felt than explained but entails the sense that we are, simultaneously, both significant and insignificant. Giving importance and majesty to both the macro units of existence as well as the micro units of existence brings us to a space that is both humble and grand at the same time. And our grandness doesn't come from an enlargement of our own drop, but from a synthesis with a grand number of other drops.

*Ubuntu* is a word that originated in southern Africa. Its meaning has evolved and differs slightly in varied regions; however, despite different evolutions of the meaning, there is a consistent essence of the word that honors community and our interdependence.

President Theodore Roosevelt alluded to the underlying principle of *ubuntu* in a speech in 1903 concerning a healthy national life: "The welfare of each of us is dependent fundamentally upon the welfare of all of us."[6]

In June 1965, the Reverend Dr. Martin Luther King Jr. summarized the essence of *ubuntu* when he addressed the graduating class of Oberlin College with these words:

> All I'm saying is simply this: that all mankind is tied together; all life is interrelated, and we are all caught in an inescapable network of mutuality, tied in a single garment of destiny. Whatever affects one directly, affects all indirectly. For some strange reason I can never be what I ought to be until you are what you ought to be. And you can never be what you ought to be until I am what I ought to be—this is the interrelated structure of reality.
>
> As Archbishop Desmond Tutu describes this perspective, ubuntu is not, "I think therefore I am." It says rather: "I am a human because I belong. I participate. I share." In essence, I am because you are.[7]

"I am because you are." This is such a powerful thought. As a mother, it is easy to see how that relates to a mother-child relationship; I would not be who I am without my children. But the reality is that each of us is interconnected in our neighborhoods, communities, and nations. We are shaped and supported by the woman standing next to us and the girl down the street.

Archbishop Desmond Tutu offered a definition in a 1999 book.

> A person with Ubuntu is . . . based from a proper self-assurance that comes from knowing that he or she belongs in a greater whole and is diminished when others are humiliated or diminished, when others are tortured or oppressed. . . .
>
> One of the sayings in our country is Ubuntu—the essence of being human. Ubuntu speaks particularly about the fact that you can't exist as a human being in isolation. It speaks about our interconnectedness. You can't be human all by yourself, and when you have this quality—Ubuntu—you are known for your generosity. We think of ourselves far too frequently as just individuals, separated

from one another, whereas you are connected and what you do affects the whole World. When you do well, it spreads out; it is for the whole of humanity."[8]

People love to talk about unity and love. We love the idea, the sentiment, and the warm feelings of love and goodwill. It feels good because it's right. Love really is the answer to reconciling differences, but the dirty business of practicing this ubuntu kind of love sometimes feels very far away from the theory of it.

On *Portlandia*, a comedy TV series, there's a sketch about a store that is crazy about putting bird pictures on things. They *love birds*. They stick bird silhouettes on lamps, embroider them on pillows, and paste them on cards. When they finish sticking birds on everything, they open the door for business and a pigeon flies in. They freak out because the bird is flying all around— then a man throws a vase at it and kills it.

The idea of something and the actual something can be two very different things. Working together as interconnected beings can be immensely satisfying and is, when discussed theoretically, an alluring and enchanting idea. However, if we allow it, our interconnectedness can also be divisive. When working as a group, it's common for competing interests to clash.

Clashes are unavoidable. Especially as an interconnected group, our decisions effect each other—a truth that is easily seen in nature. For example, the movie *I Am* explains the decision-making process of a herd of deer. One of the interviewees explained that there are competing interests within a herd of deer in making the decision of when to go to a watering hole and which hole to go to. He explains that although we might assume it is the alpha male who makes the decision, it is in fact a democratic process. One deer will look toward a certain watering hole and then another and another and as soon as 51 percent of the deer are looking in the same direction, the decision is made and they all go toward that watering hole.

The article they cite states:

> Consider, for example, a group of primates deciding where to travel after a rest period, a small flock of birds deciding when to leave a foraging patch, or a swarm of bees choosing a new nest site. In each of these cases, unless all members decide on the same

action, the group will split and its members will forfeit many of the advantages of group living. [9]

Just like the deer, every decision we women make influences the choices and opportunities of the other women around us. We all know—somewhere deep down—that the choices we make affect the whole herd. Once again, we see that we are all tied together in this great feast of life. This fact has the potential to create friction among mothers. Because we alone are not steering the direction of the herd, it may be tempting to look around and resent someone who is looking at a watering hole we really don't want to visit. There are real competing interests between us mamas. Every time we make a decision, we are, in effect, turning our heads toward a watering hole. We are casting our vote with every book we write, every item we buy, every job we take, and every choice we make.

Faced with this truth, we must make our way to another truth: right now, most mothers are simply doing the best they can with the many challenges they are handed. With this duvet cover that just never seems to fit, we all are trying to find our paths—which are now largely unmarked and often not yet even forged. There is no prescribed way. Having so many paths to choose from can be, for many, both liberating and overwhelming. This unique spot in history that we find ourselves in is creating more diversity in our experiences and lifestyles than ever before. Without as many shared experiences, it is easy to lose sight of our fundamental commonalties and the fact that, as Mother Teresa has said, "we belong to each other."

However, it becomes easier to see that being interdependent does not mean that everyone must be the same when we remember that atoms, with their protons and electrons, work so well together *because of* their differences, not in spite of them. There is a balance to be struck between being true to your community and being true to yourself. My hope is that we can agree to choose the path that leads us toward each other, remembering as we do so that we will all walk that common path in our own necessarily unique ways.

# ENDNOTES

1.  Charlie Todd, "The Shared Experience of Absurdity," filmed
    May 2011, TED Talk, 12:04, https://www.ted.com/talks/
    charlie_todd_the_shared_experience_of_absurdity/transcript?language=en.

2.  Ibid.

3.  Liz Granger, "Cancer—When Good Cells Go Bad," *The Brain Bank* (blog),
    March 11, 2013, http://thebrainbank.scienceblog.com/2013/03/11/
    cancer-when-good-cells-go-bad/.

4.  "How Do Cells Work Together in the Human Body?", *McGraw Hill
    Resources: Topic 1.3* (Whitby, Ontario: McGraw Hill Education, 2014).

5.  "Fractalism," Facebook, n.d. https://www.facebook.com/
    fractalstateofmind.

6.  Theodore Roosevelt, "Address to the New York State Agricultural Associ-
    ation" (speech, Syracuse, NY, September 7, 1903), http://www.presidency.
    ucsb.edu/ws/?pid=24504.

7.  Martin Luther King Jr., "Remaining Awake through a Great Revolution"
    (speech, Oberlin College, Oberlin, OH, June 1965), http://www.oberlin.
    edu/external/EOG/BlackHistoryMonth/MLK/CommAddress.html.

8.  Lukman Harees, *The Mirage of Dignity on the Highway of Human 'Progress': The
    Bystanders' Perspective* (Bloomington, Indiana: AuthorHouse, 2012), 73.

9.  Larissa Condradt and Timothy J. Roper, "Consensus Decision Making in
    Animals," *Trends in Ecology and Evolution* 20, no. 8 (2005).

CHAPTER 6

# Embrace Diversity

My friend, Kim, flattered me with appreciation one day when I mentioned taking my kids and some of their friends to look at the winter ice at the edges of the river that runs through our city. Speaking in front of a few women, I made sure to mention the safety precautions I took and how I talked to the kids about the dangers of winter ice beforehand. Then I added sheepishly, "There may have also been some screw drivers and hammers involved . . . but it was so interesting for the kids to chip away at some of the blocks of ice and look at the variations in different pieces of ice."

Kim laughed and said, "Wow, I bet they loved that. I never do that kind of stuff with my kids." No jealousy, no defensiveness, just a remark of pure appreciation, the way a woman would look at a patch of daffodils and think how lovely they were without for a minute wishing she could also be a daffodil.

On another day, Kim explained to me how she goes to bed early every night, because she wakes up at 5:30 every morning to exercise, meditate, make a delicious hot breakfast for her five kids, and get them all off to school on time. My jaw dropped. I felt like I was in the presence of a magical wonder. The structure, the consistency of it all—I told her how fantastical it sounded. That magic trick will never appear in my home, as marvelous as it is. And it doesn't have to. Kim and I have the pleasant opportunity to be able to appreciate how completely different we both are.

Although cooperation is an important component to village building, dealing with differences is, admittedly, not so easy. Not all of my relationships with those who are very different from me are as smooth as my friendship with Kim.

## Nature's Great Balancing Act

When I was in Mexico, my husband and I went on a hike through a subtropical deciduous forest. Whenever I go into a forest, I always feel that I am in the presence of greatness. I loved our adventure through the foreign forest with our equally foreign, machete-bearing guide. Although the forest we hiked in receives a good amount of rainfall, our guide told us, it must endure long dry periods as well. During this time of leanness, the trees will shed their leaves in order to conserve water. When trees, in mass numbers, slow down to conserve, the sunlight is able to more easily reach the forest floor. The forest is prudent and wise.

We were in the thick of the lush, dense forest where beauty, peace, and harmony seemed to be perfuming the very air around us when our guide told us about a particular tree that we had stopped at. He explained that the tree was not actually a tree, but that it was a growth that had grown over a tree, taking all the sunlight and water, eventually completely taking over and killing the tree underneath. It was an alien invasion, a hostile takeover, a military coup.

Suddenly the peaceful, tranquil forest didn't seem so docile anymore. I was surprised at how competitive and merciless nature seemed. However, nature doesn't take more than it needs to stay alive. It has a natural appetite suppressant through biodiversity. Biodiversity is vital to any ecosystem. Just as the number one rule in investment is to diversify to spread risk, so is it also important for an ecosystem to have different functions and players to step up when others become weak. A balanced ecosystem has a natural set of checks and balances. Opposition is a necessary part of nature's balancing act.

This opposition—though necessary for plants, animals, and humans—can undoubtedly be frustrating to deal with. Sometimes it is tempting to think that it would be better if something that seemed opposed to our interests were simply removed.

This was the thought of some fishermen a few decades ago who campaigned for killing whales, because they were diminishing the fish supply, thus diminishing jobs. According to *National Geographic Wild* in a program called, "A Life Among Whales," the local authorities decided to allow the fishermen to kill whales in order to increase the fish supply. To the fishermen, reducing their natural opposition seemed like a great idea.

So the fishermen started killing off the local whales, and there was more fish for them—initially.

However, the killer whales in the region, who usually preyed on younger whales, were forced to feed on other animals, such as seals. When there weren't any seals to eat, they turned to the otters.

As the killer whales feasted on otters, an unprecedented low population of otters meant that the otters' prey—urchins, crabs, abalones, clams, mussels, and snails—flourished.

In their now unprecedented large numbers, the otters' natural prey fed on and decimated the kelp forests where many fish larvae grew in relative protection.

Without the kelp forests to protect those little fish eggs, they became easy targets for a variety of sea life. In the end, there was fewer fish in the sea than there were before the fishermen got rid of those seemingly pesky whales. Contrary to the fishermen's original logic, the whales weren't competitors— they were partners. Their contribution to the diversity of sea life may have looked as though it was bringing opposition to the fishermen but, in fact, it was facilitating abundance for them.

The same phenomenon can occur among us moms when we discover differences with others and perceive those different from us as competitors bringing opposition rather than as partners offering abundance for all. There is an equally rich, abundant, and interdependent diversity among people, and part of learning to work together is learning to reach beyond tolerance toward something better and truer: appreciation.

Personality traits and ways of being that we may perceive as problems, nuisances, obstacles, or diminishing us could very well be indirectly keeping us afloat. We may in fact owe *our* very way of being to them.

As we truly learn to appreciate the diversity within our own villages and realize how our differences strengthen us, our villages will thrive, benefiting from everyone's varied skills and contributions. Embracing diversity facilitates connection.

## Our Beautiful Minds

Thomas Armstrong, PhD, author of *Neurodiversity*, looks at ADHD, autism, depression, schizophrenia, mood disorders, and mental retardation and explains the evolutionary advantages we all benefit from in having a neurologically diverse species.

> The first use of the word "neurodiversity" in print was in an article by journalist Harvey Blume published in the *Atlantic*, in September 1998. Blume wrote,
>
> "Neurodiversity may be every bit as crucial for the human race as biodiversity is for life in general. Who can say what form of wiring will prove best at any given moment? Cybernetics and computer culture, for example, may favor a somewhat autistic cast of mind."
>
> Each civilization also defines its own forms of giftedness. In ancient cultures that depended on religious rituals for social cohesion, it might have been the schizophrenics (who heard the voices of the gods) or the obsessive compulsives (who carried out the precise rituals) who were the gifted ones. Even in today's world, being at the right place at the right time seems to be critical in terms of defining whether you'll be regarded as gifted or disabled.[1]

Diversity is essential for the propagation of mankind. Understanding this can help us to more easily appreciate and love our fellow villagers. Perhaps Prince Siddhartha Gautama, the founder of Buddhism, caught the vision of this when he wrote: "When you realize how perfect everything is, you will tilt your head back and laugh at the sky."

Despite how perfect everything may look when you zoom out far enough, it may not feel so great down in the trenches. Though things may be perfect in terms of the universe at large, diversity will inevitably bring some conflict, tension, and frustration. However, embracing diversity means that we have to trust each other and respect each other's differences.

I myself am someone who is a little different. I have ADHD. It wasn't until I visited with a psychiatrist that I understood so much more about myself and about how diverse we all really are. I learned to see my differences as beneficial not only to myself but to society as a whole.

People with ADHD have less dopamine receptors than everyone else. Having low dopamine doesn't feel good, and so people with ADHD get busy trying to create experiences for themselves that increase dopamine in their brains. This works as an advantage in some ways and a disadvantage in other ways. Researchers have found that in hunter-gatherer societies, those who have less dopamine receptors are the most nourished of the group. Conversely, they found that in agrarian societies, they are the least nourished. Hunting is exciting and draws on the strengths of the ADHD brain chemistry; farming is slow-paced and favors a different kind of personality type.

I have realized that I am not broken, I just have a different skill set. People with ADHD, statistically speaking, are at a greater risk of being in prison, divorced, fired, accidentally pregnant, and addicted to drugs. Those are my people. We are also more likely to be fun, dynamic, creative, and brave. We can take risks other people wouldn't feel comfortable handling, and we crave thinking in ways no one ever prescribed for us. I may be generalizing for the sake of brevity, but my point is this: we have a skill set unique to us, and we can contribute to society in unique ways because of how we are hardwired.

This is true of everyone. We all have both macro (big-picture) and micro (individually focused) moralities. Our world would be a better place if everyone could agree on a macro morality prioritizing the value of love. Divine love is a value I wish all of humankind could embrace.

Micro moralities, on the other hand, are not absolutes. Traits that are advantageous to some people—like communication methods, forms of creativity, or learning styles—are not necessarily beneficial to others and may actually interfere with being productive in developing their own unique skill sets.

My mom is one of the most organized and efficient women I know. Her priorities are always clear, and she breezes through list making and list checking like a gettin'-'er-done wonder woman. She has also developed a micro morality for herself that supports and strengthens her skill set. She has a number of values in her micro morality. A few of her values are productivity, efficiency, order, and a calm environment. All of her values that make up her micro morality help her to develop her skills and abilities. She is fantastic at getting from A to B in an efficient and productive manner. She doesn't need to start wondering about the nature of A, whether B exists in alternate dimensions, or how folks in Zimbabwe make their way from A to B.

My micro morality looks a little different. A few of the values that strengthen my skill set are curiosity, fearlessness, creativity, truth, and wonder. I wouldn't flourish using my mom's values, and my mom doesn't need my value system in the way that it's ordered, either. She needs her own. We all do.

For years, my mom would often give me kind but confused looks whenever she saw my car filled with junk or when she saw me absorbed in some topic that had absolutely nothing to do with getting anything done. She would often say to me, "C. J., doesn't it feel so nice when your home is in order?" I could never honestly say that it did. Order and consistency and the monotony required to maintain those things actually made me feel the opposite of peaceful. They made me feel caged and restless. My mom didn't think I was seeking a peaceful life, because I don't feel peace in the same way that she feels peace. As we have both made our way to this understanding, we have been able to deepen our respect and appreciation for each other.

Major conflicts can arise when people mistakenly think that their micro morality is or should be the same as everyone else's micro morality. Avoiding this mistaken paradigm can help avert some conflict; however, even with an open mind and a thirst for understanding, we will probably never be able to completely wrap our heads around the complexity of many of the loved ones in our lives. Amid the complexity, tension is inevitable.

## From Dissonance to Harmony

Love takes patience, wisdom, and hard work. Another critical step toward practicing love is making peace with the inevitable conflict and tension that arise from connecting, sharing, and cooperating. Tension may seem not so great, and I don't personally know many people who excitedly run toward conflict and tension with others, but there has never been a great story written that didn't also include conflict and tension. The great story of your life must also include some tension if you intend it to be a classic. Cooperation among diverse individuals offers us just that.

When my sister was in high school, she performed in a music festival with her school band. After the band played, the adjudicator addressed the group to offer feedback. He was speaking to the band about the importance of tension and release in music, how powerful it is when dissonant notes create tension and that tension is relieved with a more harmonic melody.

Suddenly, he stopped talking and looked at my sister. "Excuse me," he said. My sister sat up. He continued, "Yes, *you*. I'm talking to you. I'm not sure why you think it's okay to be rude and not listen to what I'm saying, but I'm taking the time to offer some constructive criticism. The least you could do is listen to what I'm saying." My sister, who had been listening the entire time, gave him a tense look, mortified and wide-eyed. He spoke again, "I'm not serious. I know you were listening. I just wanted to make a point." My sister sighed a confused sigh of relief, and the adjudicator continued, "And there's the release."

Tension, which is often achieved in music through harmonic dissonance, is not only a vital component to any piece of music, but also a natural and necessary part of life. This will always be the case. We can't avoid tensions with others, but we can approach those tensions with love, kindness, and prayer. Practicing and embracing this type of approach can resolve our experienced dissonance and offer us a euphoric release. *Aaahhhh.*

Within a small union—a marriage, for instance—most tension arises from differences. (I'm not even talking about differences like "he loves apple pie, she loves blueberry pie." I'm talking about "he loves apple pie, and she hates apples so much that she is working day and night to ban apples in modern society." Serious differences.) It is, however, exactly those differences that are often what brought the two together in the first place. The differences balance and complete each other. This micro unit is also true in a larger sense. The differences among human beings are vital for us to survive and thrive. We are each pieces of a large puzzle. A single piece makes no sense in and of itself, but when the whole is fitted together, the picture is meaningful and complete.

With all of our diversity—all our differences in priority, energy, focus, and the unavoidable tensions that are inevitable in a healthy, diverse group—there is a unifying, harmonious song that all can hear and sing: the song of love.

Without adopting love as our deepest and truest melody, all of our differences will lead to discord, and we will remain stuck in our tensions. During times of tension, I think that if God was asked, "Whose side are you on?" his answer would be, "I'm on everyone's side." As a dear friend of mine once put it: "There is no us and them; there is only us."

# ENDNOTES

1.   Thomas Armstrong, *Neurodiversity: Discovering the Extraordinary Gifts of Autism, ADHD, Dyslexia, and Other Brain Differences* (Cambridge, MA: Da Capo Press, 2010).

# CHAPTER 7

# Women as Connectors

I was watching my oldest son play soccer the other day when suddenly the (rather intense and a little bit grumpy) coach barked, "No holding hands on the soccer field!" The instruction was directed at two little girls on Will's team who were, in fact, holding hands in the middle of the game. This is not the first time I've seen this—a few months ago during another one of Will's soccer games, I witnessed two girls on the field holding each other's hands as they twirled around and around. Why weren't they fighting for the ball? It was clear that they were simply more interested in playing with each other.

There are women who are ultra-feminine, women who are ultra-masculine, and women who lie on a spectrum between the two. Not all girls hold hands and spin around on a soccer field. Not all girls love making daisy chains or chatting about shoes. However, I still feel it valuable to acknowledge and respect some general strengths of our gender. We've inherited a legacy of being powerful creators of life, beauty, family, and love. Collectively, women have been instruments of connectedness and belonging. Throughout history, more often than not, women have been the *reason* why men have forged their stories of building, innovation, discovery, and heroism. In many cases, those stories, which dominate history books, are all just different variations of one basic storyline: the story of men striving to support and sustain the keepers of their hearts—the creators of their futures—as they've worked in tandem to raise the succeeding generation.

As women have engaged in the work of creating children, two major strengths of mothers as a group have been instrumental: the ability to connect and the ability to support cooperative work. Collectively armed with these strengths, mothers become a significant force when they flock together.

As a result of trying to protect these valuable networks of association, women can discuss relationships with nuance and extraordinary insight. Without any formal training, women often have a natural flair to be able to see the complexities of both emotions and relationships. These skills can largely be linked to our genetic and hormonal makeup.

Paul Zak found consistencies among women between hormones and having rich social networks. As the founding director of the Center for Neuro-economics Studies at Claremont Graduate University in California, Zak presented his findings about the neurological and hormonal differences between men and women at a TED conference in 2011. He explained that in over a decade of research, women have consistently been found to release higher amounts of oxytocin than men. This hormone (elevated when a woman becomes a mother) motivates social bonding and is thought by Zak to be correlated to being trustworthy, generous, compassionate, and empathic. In addition, estrogen makes women extra sensitive to oxytocin. At times when estrogen is high in a woman, her levels of oxytocin will be the most potent, as will her awareness of the quality of the relationships in her life.[1]

Due to differences in physiology, men and women react differently to problems and also have different ways of prioritizing and maintaining social relationships. As long as women are the ones who give birth to and nurse babies, we will, as a whole, always generate more oxytocin than men, which means these largely hormonally driven differences will forever remain a functional part of our reality. This reality pushes us to make relationship building a priority as we work toward building a village for ourselves.

Sarah Hrdy explains that, from an anthropological point of view, creating a network of help and support has always been such a vital task for mothers that women have evolved to be hardwired for connecting with others.

> Beginning in girlhood, and as they mature, women become increasingly adept at making friends. . . . Whether consciously or not, women seek "sisters" with whom to share care of our children.

Even the obsession with being popular and "belonging" so poignantly evident in teenage girls, rendering them both acutely sensitive to what others think and also causing them to be competitive and ruthlessly mean in excluding others, may possibly have much to do with forging bonds which in ancestral environments would have been critical for successful childrearing. . . . Girls as they matured to breeding age and throughout life needed to line up help from more individuals than just their mates. The bonds themselves became the resource to be protected.[2]

If we look at female behavior in this way—as forging bonds to develop a support system—then the behavior of the girls on Will's soccer team makes sense. The girls are already starting to build their community.

A UCLA study supports Hrdy's assertion regarding women's hardwiring. Researchers looked at stress response in a new way. Prior to the study, the researchers explained that most of the research on stress response had only been conducted on male subjects. They explained, "The rationale has been that, because females have greater cyclical variation in neuroendocrine responses (due to the reproductive cycle), their data present a confusing and often uninterpretable pattern of results."[3]

The study then focused on females and found stark differences between the male and female response. When females are faced with a stressful situation, they are less likely to exhibit the physical changes to prepare for a fight or flight response. Instead, they found that women will tend to have an oxytocin release, which is a hormone that encourages caretaking and bonding. The researchers state that what they found in women was not a "fight or flight" but "tend and befriend" response.

Females may selectively affiliate in response to stress, which maximizes the likelihood that multiple group members will protect both them and their offspring. Accordingly, we suggest that "the female stress response of tending to offspring and affiliating with a social group is facilitated by the process of "befriending," which is the creation of networks of associations that provide resources and protection for the female and her offspring under conditions of stress.[4]

This "tend and befriend" response works to our advantage. It drives us to work collectively, and as such, we can effect great changes in our villages, communities, and nations, improving the situations in which we raise our children.

An inspiring example of mothers working together for the collective good comes from JoAnn Martin, professor of sociology/anthropology and Convener of Women's, Gender, Sexuality Studies Program at Earlham College. After spending time among the people of the Mexican community of Buena Vista, she noted the powerful influence the mothers of the community had on local political issues due to their strong networks and their ability to work cooperatively to fight corruption in their local government. Martin explains in her article, "Motherhood and Power," that the women of Buena Vista became incensed at the corruption that pervaded the government. Although they did not hold positions of office, their ability to assemble, communicate, and network made their influence potent. They would gather in the square to buy bread and to share stories of local corruption, water shortages, and illegal land sales. The perception of government corruption was exposed largely because the women gathered and shared their stories.

And when they presented themselves, they did so—not as a political group—but as a group of mothers who were concerned for their families and their communities. Mamas hold a lot of clout in Mexican culture, and because these women understood their positions of power, they were able to use them to benefit their community.

Together they tore down houses that were built illegally on communal land, gathered money to help alleviate sickness, and lent money to each other to support business start-ups. They also banded together and battled government bureaucrats. One case Martin mentions was a meeting of women who gathered informally and made their way into the president of the pueblo's office for an unscheduled, informal visit. They found chairs for themselves to sit on and, with children in tow, they began to throw down their complaints. Martin states:

> The meeting began with the Maestra relating the long history of non-support from the president. . . . Another woman complained that they had asked for a septic tank in their area and nothing had

been done. The president interrupted her to say that the solution had been worked out. He described in detail what he would do . . . but Maria responded that his solution would work only for one or two years. . . . She said, "We come to you because you are the highest authority in our pueblo. . . . You are the father of our pueblo and you need to resolve our problems. We don't want promises, we want something to get done."[5]

This informal meeting lasted for over two hours.

What was true for the mothers of Buena Vista and what has always been true for mothers is that the work of mothers is greatly augmented when approached as a cooperative venture. Because of that reality, women are so often the natural leaders and experts in building strong social networks and working cooperatively. We have been biologically primed to excel in this way.

And when I think about this reality and about our mothering heritage, I can clearly see that we have the potential to collectively capitalize on our strengths as we embrace one another as a community, following in the footsteps of millions of mothers who have walked before us. We can be far more than the sum of our parts as we work together, taking pride in our shared biological passion for connecting, cooperative work, and caring for children.

# ENDNOTES

1.    Paul Zak, "Trust, Morality—and Oxytocin?", filmed July 2011, TEDGlobal, 16:34, https://www.ted.com/talks/ paul_zak_trust_morality_and_oxytocin.

2.    Hrdy, *Mothers and Others*, 271.

3.    Gale Berkowitz, "UCLA Study on Friendship Among Women: An Alternative to Fight or Flight," Anapsid.org, last modified January 1, 2014,  http:// www.anapsid.org/cnd/gender/tendfend.html.

4.    Ibid.

5.    JoAnn Martin, "Motherhood and Power: The Production of a Women's Culture of Politics in a Mexican Community," *American Ethnologist* 17, no. 3 (August 1990): 470–490, doi: 10.1525/ae.1990.17.3.02a00040.

CHAPTER 8

# Seek and Create Places to Connect

J ane Jacobs, a pioneer in urban planning, asserted that city planning should encourage community interaction. I also believe that the physical spaces we inhabit have great influence over community connection and interactions. A friend of mine shared how one of the best living arrangements she ever had was when she, her husband, and their two young children were living in married-student housing. Although the living space itself had much to be desired, their unit, along with the others, were all built around a fantastic park where the children loved playing. The families interacted quite frequently due to their shared need of the playground, which was literally just out their back doors. She and her husband both loved the close proximity and practical ease of their immediate community. So many of us, however, do not live in neighborhoods that naturally foster community connection. For those of us who find ourselves in these situations, we must seek out and create places to connect.

When we first moved back to Canada from the United Kingdom, my attempts to make friends often felt as awkward as my dating days. In fact, sometimes I would come home and tell my husband, "Hey, I picked up a chick at the library today, she seemed nice. Her kids' ages don't really match ours. . . . I *might* call her," or even, "I'm wondering if I want to take things to the next level with this girl I'm seeing—I mean, I like chatting with her at Mommy and Me playtime, but I just don't know if I want this ever to become a playdate kind of relationship." There is indeed a hook-up scene for moms, but it takes place at playgrounds and libraries rather than at bars or clubs.

A friend of mine told me that when she started having kids, she just made it a goal to go somewhere every day. Even if it was just to the grocery store, it was helpful to her to—at the very least—make a physical connection with the outside world. I think that is a great idea. However, there are places beyond the checkout line that are also worth considering.

## We're Not in Kansas Anymore

New-mom groups have their limitations, but when I was in Peterculter the local mom-and-tots group, which met weekly at the village hall, meant everything to me. It was there I met a great group of women. Our friendships flourished to the point that we started hanging out outside of mom-and-tots time. We came together for dinners, strolling castle gardens, and playdates. Those cherished friendships all came from me taking that first (often uncomfortable) step outside my flat and making my way into a room full of total strangers.

Playgroups, La Leche groups, prenatal classes, libraries, baby-and-me swim classes, Strollercize—hopefully, wherever you are living you will be able to find a group of new moms that you can connect with. There is something very satisfying about talking with other moms who are also being flung into the crazy that inevitably comes with new motherhood. When you find yourself dropped in a place that looks as foreign as the middle of Oz, it helps to seek out the other new moms who are also scrambling to navigate their way along the Yellow Brick Road. These moms have the potential to be your fellow warriors, battling alongside you to overcome all the difficulties of your new reality. My friend Felicia found this to be true when she had her first baby:

> I made three really close friends when I was pregnant with my first—we were all in this group called Birth Takes a Village. We went through pregnancy together, and we went through being moms together. We'd call each other and say, "Okay, this is happening to my child. Is this normal? Is this okay?" One night, when I was so tired I didn't even know how I could face the world, I called up one of my friends and said, "I have slept maybe two hours." My

friend said, "I've only slept an hour and a half." And together we were somehow able to laugh about it.

Getting out of the house, being with friends, and knowing I was not alone was the biggest thing for me. We'd go to Starbucks and we'd laugh. It was so great to be able to talk over things like nursing—which can be so difficult for many—because everyone has different information they can share. I don't know what I would have done without those girls. Even today, we are still a support to each other: we share stories, we share tears, we share everything. Our children are friends, and it is truly beautiful. Having these women in my life is a gift.

During pregnancy your whole body is going through these changes and it's sometimes the first time in your life that you truly learn to surrender. And then you become a mother, and surrender really screams your name. Having good friends can help you through those tough times.

—Felicia

# Hi-Dee-Ho There, Neighbor!

Getting to know the people in your proximity is important. Community schools, community soccer, or being involved in your community league (if your neighborhood has one) are a few examples of places to get to know the people who live the closest to you. Of all the mothers I know and love, the one I spend most of my time with, the one I help out the most, and receive help from the most is not the one I've known the longest or the one who I have the most in common with (or even the one who is related to me). She is the one who lives three houses down. I have met more than a few moms at libraries or stores, and we've started chatting and hit it off, but, even if both of us were village building at the time, if we lived on opposite sides of the city, the friendship would realistically be an unlikely one.

The first time I met my neighbor, we were at our local playground. Her daughter came over to the swings and asked me to give her a push, my friend then came over, and we started chatting. She has since become one of my closest friends. It warms my heart when I look out my kitchen window to see my back gate slowly open as my friend's four kids spill into my backyard and ask if they can jump on our trampoline. So many times, I have found myself at that horrible time just before supper when my own kids are tired, hungry, and looking for a fight—and then the neighborhood kids have come to my rescue as my kids rush out to the backyard to play with them.

I loved making soup with her and talking about books and recipes together. We swapped tips and stories and kept each other company while taking care of our little ones. We have needed each other many times, and every time we showed up for each other, our friendship grew. The people who live closest to you can be the best candidates for village building.

Community building often involves mothering others' children and welcoming them into your home. Living in Canada, I've found that summertime is the easiest time to welcome neighborhood kids into my circle without too much extra work, as they can play for hours in the backyard—especially when I have a number of stations (LEGO table, sidewalk chalk, trampoline) set up. Often, when we are handing out in our front yard, other children who are out riding their bikes or scooters will swing by, say hi, and play with our children for a while. During Canadian winters, community outdoor ice rinks are fantastic places for neighborhood kids to meet up and skate or play hockey.

There is wisdom in "adopting" your neighbors. This is something that I'm still working on right now, but when I can, and especially if I see toys in their yard, I make an effort to knock on neighbors' doors, introduce myself, and sometimes invite them into my home—if I feel comfortable and safe enough to do so. I also have plans to initiate a neighborhood block party so we can block off our street, allowing neighbors to spend time with one another and get to know one another in a common space.

It takes time to reach out—building relationships with anyone is a process, not an event—but the result is worth it.

From the website neighborsgathering.com, one passionate, visionary blogger shared with me part of his search to understand why we have become so alienated from each other and how to mend the breech.

As soon as I begin thinking about the reasons for our alienation from one another and from nature, my thinking becomes crowded, and I begin to realize how complex the issues are. . . . Regardless of the causes, it is obvious that something is sick and broken. I'm interested in figuring out why there's suffering, why the world is so messed up, and how we as a community can heal it. I don't have all the answers to these tough questions but I want to make a difference somehow.

My small contribution toward the healing of this broken world has been to invite and then to create a space in our home for our neighbors to gather once a week. I created a flyer, and it was tagged, "Won't you be my neighbor?" I sent the flyer to neighbors within walking distance, over a several block area. Then I established a time and introduced the idea. We told everyone that our house was going to be available for gatherings on a weekly basis from that point on.

When he was asked the question, "What changes have you seen in your life, the lives of your neighbors, and your community since you started the gatherings?" he answered that he has seen relationships form among his neighbors. And that people who had lived beside one another for years, yet didn't even know one another's names were able to learn about the others' needs, enabling them to reach out and help.

He offered the following examples of how his neighbors were able to support each other after he and his wife offered a space for everyone to gather:

Two doors down there's a neighbor whose wife recently got a job. She was unemployed for a while, so she and her husband really needed the money her new job would bring in but it meant that she had to leave her husband, who's handicapped, at home alone even though he needed help getting to doctor appointments and getting around. So there's a neighbor on the street behind us who had time available and took it upon herself to kind of be a chauffeur. She spends time, taking him to the doctor and wherever he needs to go. Now I don't know what could have been done otherwise to meet his need, but it definitely would have been more difficult without the help of his neighbor.

We also have a neighbor whose father passed away and when she had a memorial service at her home I think it was encouraging for her when a good number of neighbors showed up at the memorial service to give her comfort and support.

There's just a sense of caring that would not have been there before.

These neighbors who were once strangers now walk dogs together. They take care of one another's pets and keep an eye on one another's homes when they go on vacation.

Neighbors are not necessarily "like-minded"—the only thing we may have in common is the desire to be in a community where members can experience a sharing of life. Healing and love, acts of kindness, and a growing sense of connection to one another and our shared environment began with simply listening as each of us answers in turn, the unspoken question, "How ya doing?"

My vision is for a network of neighborhood gatherings which, I believe, have the potential to transform the world. We are experiencing the power of love in transforming our neighborhood. If what we are doing here in our neighborhood could be duplicated across the world, perhaps we could have reason to hope.

## Churches, Synagogues, Mosques—Take Your Pick

Whether it's a mosque, synagogue, church, or temple, all of these buildings have served at least one useful, basic function for hundreds, if not thousands, of years: they have offered a place for people to gather.

About a year after my youngest was born, I was very lucky that I had the opportunity to join a little organization called The Cycling Mamas. They cycle in the spring and fall, and then, in the winter, they cross-country ski and call themselves the Grace Gliders.

This mamas' group started in my neighborhood forty years ago by a group of women who attended the Grace United Church. It began as an outreach program and has helped countless mothers through life with small children. The cost for three months, every Tuesday and Thursday morning, is $35.00 plus $15.00 for each child you will be dropping off. It is so accessible, it makes my heart sing. The women come around 9:15 a.m. and drop their children off in an annex situated across a small parking lot from the church. The annex is a little, 400-square-foot, single-room building (aside from the bathroom), where there are cupboards full of toys and books for the children to use.

With the money they collect from the dues, the women are able to hire a couple of baby-sitters, lovely older ladies with grown children of their own. They love the children, and it feels so great to know that they are looking after my children. They also require the mothers to sign up for 1–3 sitting-duty days, depending on how many children they have. The women in charge are passionate about helping moms stay active and connected with other moms.

I don't belong to the Grace United Church—which is the case for most of the women who participate in the cycling group—but I have a deep respect for the people of the Grace United Church and am in awe of their generosity in facilitating the Cycling Mamas program. They truly helped mend my broken heart.

When I joined Cycling Mamas, I was desperate. I was tired and over two hundred pounds, but the idea of being able to drop my kids off and enjoy a solid hour of peace and quiet for a bargain price (and having this close to home) was a godsend. My body was so out of shape that at times, I thought maybe I was broken. I wondered if this was just my new reality after having three kids—perhaps I would never bounce back. I was timid on the trails and afraid of going too fast, which was so unlike the pre-baby me. I sadly considered that the old me, the adventurous me, the strong me, was dead.

I joined the Cycling Mamas with slight trepidation, considering my shape and how fast I heard the women bike. I found out the stories were all true—they were fast. The mamas in this group are friendly, motivated, and tough—they fly up and down the many hills within the river valley trail system here in Edmonton like it's nothing. There are three groups: the fast group, the medium group, and the slow group. I joined the slow group and didn't find them to be very slow at all. I huffed, I puffed, I wheezed my way forward, almost always the slowest of the slow. The other ladies cheered me on and without offering to ease up, they emboldened me with "You got this, C. J.," and "You're doin' great, C. J." I didn't find these words of encouragement patronizing, because I needed every single bit of positive energy I could get during those hard seventy-minute rides.

At the beginning of the season, Sharon, an experienced rider, took me under her wing and generously offered to lead the slow group. Although Sharon looked like an Olympic athlete to me on her bike, I learned that she had a journey of her own. Sharon shed a lot of weight and gained a lot of physical and emotional strength by participating in Cycling Mamas. She expressed multiple times how much this group has meant to her and how grateful she is for the happiness that has come into her life from good health. And as she changed her lifestyle, she was also able to help her husband and children lead active lifestyles. She is an inspiration to all of the women in the group and is committed to helping other mothers.

I have a love-hate relationship with hills. On my first ride up a long hill, I remember Sharon cycling beside me, cheering me on. Sharon taught me about gearing down so that the hill would be doable. And she taught me the trick of gearing up before the hill to gain momentum before gearing down. She taught me about trying to keep an even cadence as I cycle and, like a prophetess, predicted that my bottom really would quit hurting after a few rides. Whenever I would reach the top of a hill, Sharon would always cheer for me, along with everyone else who made it up.

On another bike ride early in that first season, I was struggling up a long hill and everyone passed me except for one woman who could have passed me as well, but instead said to her friend, "You go ahead, I want to stay beside C. J." At one point, she was beside me and Sharon was on the other side, and I felt as though I were being escorted by angels.

The extensive trail system which exists throughout the beautiful river valley is quite special, and we are very lucky to have a trail system that has been built along the river and through beautiful wooded areas.

After a long winter here in Canada, the almost unbelievable miracle of spring comes. The snow melts away, the grass turns from a dead yellow to a vibrant green, and nature explodes triumphantly as though the earth were rising from the dead. The transformation from the dark dead of winter to the vibrant sunny green spring reminded me on my first bike ride of the season that our bodies also have the potential for regeneration. This group offered that opportunity for me. It changed everything. I was welcomed into the group with open arms by all, but especially by the mothers who ran the group. They kept encouraging me and helping me.

Women who had been in the group years ago show up a couple of times a season to give lessons to those of us who have no clue what we are doing. They do so because they love the group and what it gave them when they were struggling with small children. The group has been an invaluable resource for mothers for four decades and has offered much needed respite from the isolation of staying home with children.

When we finish our ski or ride, we come back to the annex and have a snack and chat together. I love the feeling of camaraderie that is so easily built by women who are largely in the same stage of life and who love to ski and cycle. We talk about waxing skis, the times we fell down, how to prevent your chain from falling off, and how to gear down on those tough hills. We have so much in common from our shared experiences exercising.

There is something magical that happens between people when they struggle side-by-side and when they stay with you during hard times. A weakness of many mom-and-tots groups is that moms just get together to chat, and although we connect, it is a more superficial connection than what comes from people who work together and solve problems together and sacrifice for one another.

The Cycling Mamas group started from a few women, meeting at church, who decided to do something to help support the moms in their neighborhoods. And while no religious institution is perfect (because they all are comprised of imperfect human beings), it is my belief that most who attend are just trying to do their best to nurture love and goodness in their lives. Religious groups are great places to learn about love, forgiveness, grace, and mercy— big themes when it comes to relationship building. Good churches reach out and can serve as places where community and connection are fostered. My own consistent church attendance has not only fed me spiritually on dark days but has also offered me a place where I have been able to develop meaningful friendships and where I have found some of my most treasured villagers.

## There's No Place Like Home

Over the past year, I've worked really hard on opening my own doors (both front and back) to help others feel welcome. It's the neighborhood kids who usually knock on my back door to ask if they can play with our kids in the backyard. It's other mothers who usually knock on my front door to drop their kids off for a swap or come in for a chat. We've had to step up the cleaning a bit and maybe lower our standards as well, but it has been worth the company.

Welcoming people into my home and our family life is a refreshing act, like digging a river to flow in and out of a pond to bring fresh water in and avoid the stink of stagnant water. Others can bring fresh ideas, fresh perspectives, fresh jokes, and fresh enthusiasm.

There are those times in your mothering career when your house may look fairly consistently like a nuclear test site. Even then, open those doors of yours, hold your head up high, and let the people in anyhow. Maybe they will think a little less of your housekeeping. Who cares? It's a small trade-off for the value that inviting other people into your space will bring. Don't wait for your house or your life to look perfect before you start your village building. (Hint: if you're looking to make new friends and are worried about the state of your house, look for a woman with a lot of kids and crazy hair. Chances are she won't even bat an eye.)

Last year, I became friends with a Mexican woman. We got to talking about food, and she asked if I liked Mexican food. When I answered an emphatic yes, she said she would cook for me sometime. I jumped at the chance and invited her over to our home—we would have a potluck. She accepted the invitation to my home, but refused the idea of a potluck. "No, you will not cook anything. We will bring everything." She insisted—what could I do? I knew that she had a few other friends from Mexico and told her to bring them along as well. That night my doorbell rang, I opened my door and I swear that there were twenty people standing there, holding pots of food.

I have a small home.

I have six chairs at my dinner table.

And yet none of them seemed to mind one bit. At one point in the evening, I apologized to my guests because I saw that some of them were standing while eating, and they said so casually, "No, it's nothing. In Mexico, we have big get-togethers all the time, and we are used to standing around while we eat. We don't worry about having enough chairs." That was a big moment for me: I realized that I had set limitations on my small house that didn't need to exist. I had *such* a great time that night. Great fun, great food, great people. No stagnant water that night.

# CHAPTER 9

# Develop Your Inner Mystic

Martha Beck once wrote that, in studying role conflict in American women, she had only ever met four types of women. "I found that women fell into one of four categories: those who'd chosen career (and were very conflicted); those who put family first (and were very conflicted); those who'd combined work and family (and were very, very conflicted); and mystics."[1]

I've been privileged to have met a few of these mystic women—those who are able to somehow rise above myriad conflicting messages women hear all the time about how they *should* be living their lives. The mystics are the ones who know their path—they know it from some deep, sacred place inside them, and because their decisions come from this strong place, they are able to walk their path with clarity and confidence.

*Merriam-Webster* has a few definitions of mysticism to choose from. The definition that most resembles how I have experienced mysticism in my own life is: "the belief that direct knowledge of God, spiritual truth, or ultimate reality can be attained through subjective experience (as intuition or insight)."[2] If you do not believe in God, perhaps as you read, you can stretch to believe in spiritual truth or an unseen, ultimate reality that can only be understood through the heart and mind of one who desires truth and light. Ultimately, my hope is that a diverse group of women from varied religious and spiritual backgrounds will be able to find some common ground here and connect with the thoughts in this chapter in a meaningful and helpful way.

Working with the definition above, it is easy to see that the idea of mysticism has tantalized people since the beginning of time. In Judaism, Islam, and Christianity, the beginning of us all lies with Adam and Eve. Despite differences in interpretation and some details of the story, all three of those major religions teach that humankind's first story is one where God's intelligence, presence, and involvement were key. They all believe that direct knowledge of God, spiritual truth, and ultimate reality was something that even the first people on Earth had access to. Also, in all three of those religions, there are common stories of divine shortcuts to knowledge and understanding.

Judaism, Islam, and Christianity all believe that God spoke to Noah and gave him some inside information (a great flood was coming). Neither the Old Testament nor the Quran state that Noah had weather satellites in his backyard—yet Noah knew something big was coming. It was inspiration rather than information that led him to action. Although everyone else thought Noah was crazy, he started building a giant boat on dry land and gathering an absurd amount of animals.[3] Regardless of whether you read this story literally or figuratively, the message from this ancient source is the same: people can connect with the divine to receive direction and guidance for their lives, and God can save you when it seems like there is no way out.

In the Old Testament, Queen Esther, newly married to King Ahasuerus of Persia, learned that the king's highest official, Haman, had convinced the king that all Jews should be exterminated. Being Jewish herself and afraid for the fate of her people, she asked all the Jews to fast and pray for three days for God to save her people. At the end of those three days, Esther knew what she needed to do. She boldly invited King Ahasuerus to a feast, disclosed the fact that she was Jewish, and exposed Haman's self-serving plot as a way to dispose of Esther's cousin—whom Haman despised. As a result of following divine guidance, Esther was able to change the king's mind and save her people from genocide.[4]

Another example of humankind reaching for the heavens can be found in the story of how Prince Siddhartha left his palace of wealth and comfort to find truth and wisdom. Siddhartha embarked on a quest to find enlightenment from a power greater than his own. As Siddhartha sat under a Bodhi tree, he committed to stay there and meditate until he received the light and knowledge he was seeking. He found what he was looking for and became the wise Buddha, who inspires peace and right living for millions of people. He sought "spiritual truth, or ultimate reality" and attained wisdom "through subjective experience (as intuition or insight)."[5]

Like Noah, Esther, and Prince Siddhartha, Swami Vivekananda, an Indian Hindu monk, also believed that a truth exists beyond what ordinary man can see. Vivekananda described Rishis—men who were able to see this invisible truth—as "Mantra-drashtâs" or "the seers of thought." He said, "The truth came to the Rishis of India—the Mantra-drashtâs, the seers of thought—and will come to all Rishis in the future, not to talkers, not to book-swallowers, not to scholars, not to philologists, but to seers of thought."[6]

In the Jewish faith, there is a branch of study—Kabbalah—which turns to a collection of writings called the Zohar to learn how to access mysticism. People in Christianity strive for this divine guidance through prayer. Buddhists use meditation and yoga and have their own sacred texts to guide them toward enlightenment. Islam has its Sufis. These religions all have something more than just a code of behavior to offer—they have a hope for and a belief in the mystical.

Mysticism is very personal. Connecting with the divine is not about looking around to see what other people are doing. It is not searching for your answers in a rule book. It is a process of learning how to listen and what to listen to. It is living your life with reasonable and intelligent thought, yet, at the same time, being open to the whisperings of the wind, to those mystical pullings or pushings that may seem illogical to others—for "those who hear not the music think the dancers mad."[7]

At times, there can be those who confuse inspiration from God with a mental illness or one's own deep, unhealthy impulses—some even claim that there are dark forces, which can confuse truth seekers. Figuring out what is inspiration and what is not can be complicated. It is also a very personal journey, but broadly and simply put, my definition of mysticism is being able to hear and understand the music of heaven; *any inspiration you receive that is not filled with love is not from God.* Cultivating your spirituality and discerning what divine love really looks like takes time and is a practice.

I have tried, for most of my life, to be able to hear the music that generously plays for the mad dancers of this world. I'm not perfect at it—sometimes when the music is a blaring jazz beat, I'm spinning around in a waltz. Despite my missteps, I can see that with earnest practice over the years, I have become a better dancer. And having that access to inspiration has been invaluable in my efforts to gather a village for myself.

I understand if this sounds like a trip too arduous for exhausted, busy moms to take. However, embarking on it can open doors of happiness and guidance, not only for you but also for your children.

In 2015, an article appeared in *Maclean's* magazine entitled "The Science is in: God is the Answer." According to the findings of Lisa Miller, the director of clinical psychology at Columbia University's Teachers College, spirituality is a statistically significant factor in the well-being of adolescents.

> Spirituality, if properly fostered in children's formative years, will pay off in spades in adolescence. An intensely felt, transcendental sense of a relationship with God, the universe, nature or whatever the individual identifies as his or her "higher power," she found, is more protective than any other factor against the big three adolescent dangers. Spiritually connected teens are, remarkably, 60 per cent less likely to suffer from depression than adolescents who are not spiritually oriented. They're 40 percent less likely to abuse alcohol or others substances, and 80 percent less likely to engage in unprotected sex.[8]

According to the article, these findings are consistent among various major world religions. The article also mentions a 2005 study showing teens who had a personal relationship with God were 70 percent less likely to move from substance dabbling to substance abuse. A crucial point mentioned was that insincere involvement in church attendance or family prayer had no protective influence at all; the teens had to be personally committed to having a relationship with God for their spiritual practice to make a difference in their lives.[9]

A committed spiritual practice doesn't just help out teens. Having a relationship with God can strengthen *all* people and can affect their ability to make positive choices in their lives. The I Ching states: "The wind blows over the lake and stirs the surface of the water, thus visible effects of the invisible are manifested." Mothers who are sincerely looking for support, strength, and wisdom through spiritual practice can also benefit from many visible effects of the invisible.

I have offered the idea that we mothers need a different structure in society. We would benefit from political change and a rethinking of our physical environments. However, no change—regardless of how brilliant or well thought out—will bring peace, happiness, or satisfying community to mothers without the divinely inspired, unifying power of love. Moments of mysticism happen when your love song and the love song of the universe sync up. According to D. J. Moores, "Mysticism, then, is the perception of the universe and all of its seemingly disparate entities existing in a unified whole bound together by love."[10]

Being able to access that powerful mystic current of harmony and love can help us to connect to others in a profound, meaningful, and deeply satisfying way. Great Spirit, Allah, Jehovah, the Alpha and Omega, Yahweh, Elohim, Creator, Power Greater Than Ourselves, Brahma, God—whatever the name, all refer to an ultimate source of light and love. God is a great beating heart who yearns for all our hearts to beat with his. Each time we access the love of God through prayer, meditation, service, and the reading of sacred texts, we have the opportunity to see how He sees for a moment. When we connect to Him, we connect to the stars in the sky, the leaves on the trees, the waves of the oceans, and the bee nestled in a flower. Because God is aware, concerned, and deeply connected with every person on earth, when we connect to him, we connect to all.

> Love is the healing balm that repairs rifts in personal and family relationships. It is the bond that unites families, communities, and nations. Love is the power that initiates friendship, tolerance, civility, and respect. It is the source that overcomes divisiveness and

hate. Love is the fire that warms our lives with unparalleled joy and divine hope."[11]

There is magic in a life lived dedicated to being connected to the spirit of God. Being a mystic—taking time to connect with something greater, much greater, than you—not only helps you to connect with others but also helps you to be one of those women who are able to transcend the craziness of life and know with a firmness and calmness which path they should be walking.

I had a dream when I was living in Oxford, England, that helped me understand this. When I moved there, I had just married and had no other business bringing me to Oxford. I eventually found employment in a soap shop and then at a bank, but there were a few occasions when I found myself in the company of smart, driven people, and I shrunk a little in my own eyes, doubting my purpose. This dream I had brought me an incredible amount of confidence, and it still brings me comfort when I think of it.

In my dream, I was on one side of a vast wilderness. And I knew I was there to cross it. There were women lined up in the same way a group of runners line up for a race—I and every other woman had a course of her own in front of her, tailored to her own needs and abilities. Just as I was about to embark, I looked beside me, and a few meters away I saw a strong, fascinating woman. I looked at her and immediately thought that I wanted to follow her. I left the path in front of me and stealthily followed her.

She was fast and could journey her path without too much trouble, but soon I lost sight of her and came to a point in her path that I could not cross. It was too much for me, and I was lost and stuck. I was scared and looked around, panicked. Then a man appeared. He was a guide who was indigenous to the area. He spoke to me and asked, "C. J., what are you doing here?"

I replied desperately, "I don't know, I don't know." He told me to turn around and go back. He told me to go back to my path, the one that was laid out in front of me from the start and to follow it without worrying about how anyone else was crossing this wilderness. So I went back to my path. And then I woke up.

I have leaned on the wisdom in this dream countless times as I have tried to stay true to my own path through life. It was like God was saying to me,

"C. J., honey, just keep your eyes on your own work." One woman might be tying up her hiking boots because she has a mountain to climb, but the woman next to her might be putting on flippers and swim goggles because she has an ocean to cross. It would be bad news if the woman who had a mountain ahead of her decided that her friends' flippers looked so cool that she ditched her hiking boots, unaware of and unprepared for what lay ahead.

Since having this dream, I have been blessed to meet fellow mystics in training who remind me to continually touch base with the spiritual strength available to us all. One mystic in training I know phoned me out of the blue one day and told me that she had a free day that day and felt impressed to bring me and my family dinner that night. I was having a particularly tough day due to a pinched nerve in my neck, and when she brought me dinner she also brought kindness, strength, and insight. I needed her that day . . . and without my telling her, she somehow knew.

Another mystic in training was in a temple quietly sitting when she felt impressed to go back to school and then back to work, even though she had wanted to stay home with her young children. She kept feeling these impressions each time she visited her temple and, like a good mystic, followed the impression. Her husband was later diagnosed with cancer and died, leaving her to support her family—which she was prepared to do.

These women were stronger and better for listening to inspiration, trusting God to guide their paths. Mystics are those who are willing to completely turn their lives over to God or that higher power, and as they continually practice asking the big, old, wise universe where they belong in this great mess of life, they will be guided in the right direction.

A singularly powerful example of this concept came from a friend of mine who was, at one time, faced with a choice to continue in a fulfilling but demanding career path or to step out for a while to start a family. She shared, "If you humble yourself enough to sincerely pray and ask God which course of action is the right one for you—whatever the answer is— you can feel safe in following the answer. The end." And that's exactly how she made her decision.

Being connected to God does not mean you will avoid suffering. It does mean that you will be guided and strengthened in your efforts to love, support, and connect with the people in your life. Mysticism is what can turn black-and-white relationships into 3-D, full-color experiences when it comes to village building.

A mother I interviewed shared the following story of how God showed up for her during a particularly difficult time in her life. There was no burning bush, no parting of the seas; God whispered to the people in her life, and, like vibrant mystics, they followed the music to her doorstep.

## Julie's Tulips

My husband went to jail for sexually abusing our daughters—nobody knew about it. During the trial, we had to keep it really quiet. In the midst of the trial, a friend who didn't know about my situation dropped off an essay that she had printed off the Internet for me called "Family Crucibles." A crucible is something that they heat steel in to pull out all the impurities, so a family crucible is a trial that heats everybody to the boiling point and pulls out all the impurities.

After handing me the article, she opened up and shared that she and her husband had been so excited for the birth of their first child. When their baby was born, he had severe mental and physical deformities. She paraphrased the essay, "Welcome to Holland" by Emily Perl Kingsley (about Kingsley's experience of raising a child with a disability), and told me that was exactly how she felt. Her experience was just as Kingsley described; it was like planning a trip to Italy: they learned the language and researched Italian culture—Michelangelo, Di Vinci, etc.—they bought their tickets, and metaphorically got ready for the trip. When the baby was born it was like landing in Holland; they didn't know the language and didn't know the culture. It was slower moving, and they kind of had their hearts set on Italy. Despite the disorientation, she said they eventually found that you start noticing how Holland has its own kind of beauty. It's slower moving, but the tulip fields are beautiful.

My friend's story resonated with me. I, too, felt like in my hardship I had landed in Holland. I didn't know the language or anything about that place. I had signed on for happily ever after, and I didn't get happily ever after. The picture of Holland's tulips stuck with me, and I also thought how the word *tulips* reminded me of *two lips*, and it's like a kiss from God. Tulips became my favorite flower.

More than once during that time, I remember thinking, "Welcome to Holland." Three days after I heard the story of the tulips, a different friend of mine brought me a bouquet of tulips—in February! Who has tulips in February? She just dropped them off at the house, totally unrelated. So for a long time my daughter and I would say, "Well, welcome to Holland," every time something came up that was hard. . . . there's always tulips.

—Julie

There were three mystics in Julie's story: the woman who brought the essay, the woman who brought the tulips, and Julie herself. These women were able to be instruments of the Divine's efforts to support Julie during a heart-wrenching time in her life. I think Julie's story beautifully illustrates that building satisfying connections with others is one of the top priorities of heaven.

As a mystic, you can invoke a blessed village life upon your house, allowing God—the great mediator of all—to help us to recognize the people crossing our paths that we are meant to connect with. God can orchestrate all the lessons of experience that we need in order to learn how better to love the people in our lives. He can also inspire us to reach out and serve others in a most efficient way, because God sees what we cannot. Mystics aren't just robed men with long beards who meditate on mountain tops—they can also be found driving minivans on their way to soccer practice with bits of oatmeal on their shirt.

Mystics are the ones who have open and seeking hearts.

# ENDNOTES

1.  Martha Beck, "Yes? No? Maybe? How to Make Decisions," *Creating Your Right Life* (blog), September 29, 2013, http://marthabeck.com/2013/09/how-to-make-decisions/.

2.  Merriam-Webster.com, s.v. "mysticism," www.merriam-webster.com/dictionary/mysticism.

3.  Genesis 6–8 (King James Version).

4.  Esther 4–9 (King James Version).

5.  Barbara O'Brien, "Prince Siddhartha: The Prince Who Became the Buddha," AboutReligion, http://buddhism.about.com/od/Gautama-Buddha/fl/Prince-Siddhartha.htm.

6.  "The Complete Works of Swami Vivekananda," WikiSource, https://en.wikisource.org/wiki/The_Complete_Works_of_Swami_Vivekananda/Volume_3/Lectures_from_Colombo_to_Almora/The_Work_before_us.

7.  Aiki Flinthart, *The Yu Dragon* (Amazon Digital Services, Inc., 2012).

8.  Brian Bethune and Genna Buck, "The Science Is In: God Is the Answer," *MacClean's*, March 2015, 45, http://www.macleans.ca/society/science/god-is-the-answer/.

9.  Ibid.

10. D.J. Moores, *Mystical Discourse in Wordsworth and Whitman: A Transatlantic Bridge* (Leuven, Belgium: Peeters Publishers, 2006), 34.

11. Dieter F. Uchtdorf, "The Love of God," October 2009, transcript and video, 19:43, The Church of Jesus Christ of Latter-day Saints general conference, www.lds.org/general-conference/2009/10/the-love-of-god?lang=eng.

CHAPTER 10

# Befriend Grandmothers, Older Girls, and Aunties

I n all traditional cultures, especially those foraging societies that still exist today in more untamed parts of the world, the family is never seen as simply mother, father, and children. In cultures (past and present) that do not swim in affluence, as we do today, the extended family is and has been a vital net that serves as a support for all the children growing up under its umbrella. The family is considered to be comprised of grandmother, grandfather, aunts, uncles, cousins, mother, father, and children. The allomothers have just as important a role to play as the parents. Mothers have always relied on others to help them raise their young.

Sarah Hrdy explains the crucial role grandmothers, aunts, and older girls (like older daughters, cousins, or nieces) have played in the human race surviving and thriving, as she notes the relatively significant amount of time and energy it takes to raise a child compared with other primates.[1] This has shaped my thoughts on the importance of mothers connecting and working together—as they participate alongside fathers—in the great work of raising children.

When resources are scarce or there are difficult challenges, allomothers can have an enormous impact on the lives of the children in their family network. For so many mothers and fathers in different countries around the world, the alloparents are a part of the parenting team. Although the supporting role of an involved grandparent or aunt may not seem so important, for millions of parents over thousands of years, alloparent support has been nothing less than essential.

For the most part, alloparent support has consisted of grandmothers, older girls, and aunts. This is important to remember. Although I have been lifted by every single one of my mom friends, I have realized that mom friends are most likely flailing around and feeling like they are sinking just as much as I am. This does not mean that a symbiotic relationship cannot exist. It definitely can, but it is important to remember that a friendship with a fellow mother in the muck will probably not be able to support all of your needs and you, most likely, will not be able to support all of hers.

In addition to meeting a mom's needs, allomothers also help to meet the needs of children. Even when fathers are matching the mother's time and energy, children would benefit from a broader net. Undoubtedly, children need their parents, but they also benefit from having more than just two committed caregivers in their lives. This is why grandmothers, aunties, and older girls are *essential* pieces in the motherhood puzzle.

I know how delicious it is to meet someone like-minded—someone who easily gets where you're coming from. Often, these people are at the same place in life as you. However, I think it's important to look beyond that when gathering your village members. Motherhood offers you an opportunity to go deep and diverse in your connections with others.

## Golden Girls

I have an incredible mother who swoops into my life every time it seems like everything is falling apart. During my last pregnancy, she was really the only person in my life who I knew I could count on. I am so grateful for how much she helped me, my husband, and my children by coming and being a bright light and breath of fresh air when I felt like I was losing my mind. We definitely needed her shot of positivity during those times when no one seemed to be having a good time. I think living closer to her during my difficult time would have helped out even more, but despite the physical distance between us, my mom did everything she could to make me a priority in her life. I love her so dearly for that.

I asked her to write something about how she feels about being a mother and grandmother, and she sent this to me:

> I am now a grandmother. I travel to visit/stay with my daughters and grandchildren. I was there to help and support my daughters each time they had their babies. I go visit whenever they need me and often when they don't. And now I have beautiful grandchildren who are so precious to me. What a wonderful, new experience this is. It gives me comfort to know that I can be there for my children and grandchildren. That I can still read stories, kiss their hurts better, find worms in the garden, go to the zoo, go for walks, and do all the fun things I did with my own children. I can help my daughters paint their house, make meals when needed, and babysit the grandchildren. I am still able to help and support however they need me.
>
> I want to be a part of their lives—to feel needed and loved. I want to know of their struggles. I want to laugh with them, cry with them, and love life with them. Being a mother and grandmother has been a beautiful gift to me, which I will always cherish.

Not all moms have the luxury of a grandmother who is able to help them. In those cases, it is sometimes possible to find family substitutes through informal adoption. There may be a nonrelative who is the perfect person for your village, because they are looking for a village to belong to as well. Perhaps she's that older lady who lives down the street or that teenage girl you know who has some extra time on her hands.

Older ladies may be lonely and just as much in need of community as you. Many would be delighted to be in the company of little ones. An older woman in my church, whose children are no longer babies, always seems to have a baby in her arms. Like an adopted grandmother, she holds babies while their moms are getting food at a potluck or while they are playing the piano at church or really whenever she can get her hands on one, because she just loves babies.

One day a few months ago, when I was out for a walk, I knocked on one of my neighbors' doors, introduced myself to an older woman, and told her how much I loved her flower garden. We talked gardening for a little while, and she seemed genuinely pleased with the contact. After summer ended, she stopped by my home and handed me some seeds she had collected for me from her flowers and told me how to plant them. I think we were both more blessed by the contact than shared seeds.

I want to share some stories from women who have benefited from connecting with the older women that they've adopted into their lives.

> Mrs. Evans? She's a saint. She saved our marriage, she saved our sanity, and she got me down from three Diet Pepsis to maybe one Diet Pepsi a day. She says in so many ways, "Everything will work out." She doesn't get upset about anything.
>
> Mrs. Evans is a sweet lady in her eighties. When we moved to Irving, she was one of the first people we met. She asked, "So what can I do to help you?" like Mary Poppins. She lives right across the street; I have a saint living right across the street from me.
> —Sadie

> I was going crazy one day, as you sometimes do as a mom, and this older woman we knew took my kids to a movie. She said, "I need children time and my children and grandchildren live too far away, so can I take your kids for a while and get my fix?" And my kids still remember that so many years later.
>
> —Amanda

> Even thinking about her makes me tear up. She just was so sweet I don't even know where to start with her. Four years ago, it was really overwhelming to think of having two sets of twins, and just

thinking about how she stepped into my life at such a difficult time makes me so emotional. She really helped me when I needed help.

 I guess it really all started one day when I confided in her that I was having a really hard time knowing that we were having twins again—both sets boys. And she just stepped into my life and helped. When I was on bed rest, I was feeling really sorry for myself. I was just feeling miserable, and she would come over a lot, bring me movies and treats, and try to lift my spirits. She was so thoughtful toward me and helped to make me feel better in a really quiet, sweet way. She would even help me get all the kids ready for church and in the car on Sunday mornings because my husband had to leave early Sunday mornings because of his church responsibilities. On Monday, Wednesday, and Friday mornings, she would drive the older twins to preschool and she would stay the whole two and a half hours because parents were supposed to help clean up lunch. Also, sometimes after we had put all the kids down, she would come over and babysit for us so my husband and I could have a night out.

I have never had somebody consistently serve me like that and show that kind of love—it was just really wonderful! I get so emotional when I talk about her. She made me want to try harder to serve other people, too. She changed my life.

—Ellen

Her name is Rose. Ever since I got pregnant with my fifth, she's offered to come and clean for me or cook for me and watch the kids for me, so I could have a nap. She would babysit, so I could go to appointments. Whatever she can do for me, she does. I really believe that she was inspired many times to reach out to me.

One day I was having a meltdown, and she called me and reassured me. I'll never forget that phone call because I was feeling like such a terrible mother, and I had no one else I could say that to, no one I felt close enough to that I could share how I felt. It meant so much

to me that she called me and reassured me and pointed out all my
strengths and the good things that I do for my children.

—Raina

# Big Sister to the Rescue

A friend of my sister once remarked, "Every baby should come with a nine-year-old girl." This friend has a nine-year-old girl neighbor who loves to come over to hang out with her baby while she is busy with other tasks. Older girls, especially those just emerging from being little girls but not yet having hit the older teen years, are perfect matches for moms with babies. The idea of a baby is still for them a romantic notion which hasn't yet lost any luster with the realization of how much work is involved in taking care of them. There are many teenage girls whose eyes also light up at the thought of playing with young kids.

A French-speaking friend of mine told me that a neighborhood teenage girl wanted to improve her French, so a few times a week the girl would come over and practice her French. She would play and talk with the French-speaking children, freeing my friend to make supper and tidy up.

I remember fondly how one of my piano students was smitten with my daughter when she was born and was extremely eager to spend time with her. I wish I had invited her into my home more. I was reluctant because I thought it would be taking advantage of her, but one day her mother told me that her daughter was wanting to start babysitting and, although she wasn't old enough yet, would love the opportunity to gain unpaid experience. I guess you could say that she was looking for an internship and perhaps would have even benefited from an additional mentor. I did eventually take her up on the offer and am glad that I did as I now often call her to babysit for me.

My sister-in-law recently had her own epiphany about teenage girls at a park with her two-year-old son and two-month-old baby girl:

> After being at the park for a while, my two-month-old started to
> squirm and fuss. I knew it was time to leave, but my two-year-old
> didn't want to. I recognized the signs of pre-meltdown and was

unsure how I was going to handle a toddler tantrum and a crying baby. Panicked, I looked around and saw a large group of eleven- to thirteen-year-old girls sitting on some bleachers nearby. I simply asked one of them who seemed sweet to hold my baby while I wrangled my toddler. She was so happy to do it! The other girls were saying things like, "You're so lucky!" as they gathered around to admire the baby. A minute later, I carried a kicking and crying toddler back to the playground area, got him settled in his stroller, and rolled him back toward his sister, who was still being adored by the girls.

When I returned, I commented on how happy my baby looked and thanked the one holding her for taking such good care of her when I really needed it. I then lifted my baby up and the girl carefully released her. I settled her into her carrier and just stayed there a moment enjoying how good we all felt. As I lingered, the girls started sharing so many things with me: "I have a little baby sister," "My little sister likes to carry our baby brother and run around the house," "She's so cute."

We chatted and beamed and talked. My toddler started to fuss a little—alone and strapped in his stroller to the side of us. I looked over at him but stayed where I was, simply commenting that Taylor was lucky and that he's a great big brother who likes to hold her, too. The girl we had met first over in the playground went over to my toddler. She talked to him, commented on his snack, made him laugh, and gave him some attention. I stayed another minute or so as we enjoyed each other's company, then thanked them again, and left.

I felt happy as I walked away, knowing that I had given them an opportunity to feel useful, and it warmed my heart to see how eager they were to help me.

—Taylor

Finding an older girl who would love nothing more than to come over to your house and snuggle with your baby while you get stuff done is as lucky as finding out you have oil on your land.

An added bonus for both parties is the opportunity for an older woman to mentor the younger woman. The transition from girl to woman is fraught with stormy seas. Your wisdom and encouragement could really make a difference in her life. Obviously you wouldn't want to overstep with parents—hold off on trying to convince her how amazing her life would be if she ran away and joined the circus—but most parents would appreciate some backup, like mentioning how important it is to always try your best in school or to make smart choices with her future self always in mind or how worthwhile *she* is during what can be a pretty demoralizing time in a young woman's life.

## When Mary Poppins Drops In

Considering the ups and downs of motherhood, overall I can easily say that I love being somebody's mom. Motherhood is great and terrible and life altering and soul stretching and sprinkled with equal portions of bliss and anguish. It's intense.

Being an auntie is simpler—being an auntie is *fun*. I have nieces and nephews who love me, and I don't even have to do that much work to get their adoration. I can give fun presents, listen to their jokes, tell them outrageous stories that delight them, and leave it to their parents to deal with the really tough stuff.

When I was young, none of my aunts lived close to us, but we would connect with them at Christmastime. My aunts were all extremely important to me, and they influenced me in ways they don't even know about. I was emboldened by their strength. I paid attention to how they met tough times with a generous sense of humor. I basked in any attention they paid me. Now I get to be an auntie, and I understand my position of influence. If you can stockpile some aunties to your arsenal of alloparents, your children will be better for it.

Women with or without children can make great aunties. However, women without children of their own may have a bit more time, energy, and patience to spend on your children. These women are gold.

One woman shared with me how important a particular aunt has been in her life:

> I have an aunt who had no children of her own. Even though she lived abroad for most of my childhood (China, Korea, Pakistan, Colombia) and calls Ottawa her home, there is no other aunt so dear to me. She would send postcards and birthday cards. And when she visited us, she took us to the ballet and walked me to school. Even now, in her seventies, she sends Valentine, Halloween, and birthday cards to my kids, and always calls on my wedding anniversary. Even my parents don't do that. I am so lucky to have her.

Here are a couple of comments from some fabulous aunties:

> I love being an auntie. I felt a connection with my oldest niece even before she was born. I woke up in the middle of the night the same time my sister was giving birth, and I just knew without getting a phone call or an e-mail that my niece was being born. The first time I saw her face, it felt like she belonged to me in a way—the love that I felt in my heart was immense and even now it brings me to tears thinking about it.

> I now have two nieces, and still feel that unconditional love for them. And that's what I get from them as well. It's an amazing, nonjudgmental, pure love. I feel a strong connection to both of my nieces. I am currently in a same-sex relationship, which sometimes causes friction with other members of my family, but when I am with my nieces there is never any judgment, they just love me for who I am. It's so nice to spend time with them and to have fun and play with them—it's a wonderfully uncomplicated relationship. I have always been a fun and playful person, and my nieces have helped me to connect with that part of myself again; they've lit that spark for me and rekindled the joy.

> I think laughter is a universal language, and when I can make them laugh or they make me laugh, it's very connecting; we're making a memory together. Because I understand their sense of humor, and they understand my sense of humor, it feels like there is a part of

me in them. They bring joy to my life like nothing else. Sometimes life can get hard for me, and if I ever get down, or have a bad moment when I feel like I don't have a community or that no one understands me, I think about them. I want to be the auntie that is there for them when they have a problem, and I want to live my life in a certain fashion so that they can feel good about coming to me for help or advice. When I have those depressing moments I think back to them and remember that someone does love me, and I remember how much I love them.

—Anna

And from another auntie:

We did try to have kids years ago, but there were some problems and I couldn't get pregnant. I thought maybe I was getting too stressed out about it, and I was also feeling really stressed at work. So we decided to just step back in our efforts and just wait and see. I'm the youngest in my family and I have siblings who all have wonderful children, so I decided to fill my time with them. We threw ourselves into our roles as aunt and uncle, and I loved being able to have the time to develop a close relationship with my nieces and nephews. I was also able to be the chilled-out, fun adult in their life, something that maybe isn't so easy to be as a parent.

I loved being an auntie so much that I began to help out other mothers who also seemed to need some backup. I was asked to babysit and not only did I jump on those chances to help, but I also made a big effort to have a lot of fun with the kids in my life. I am very young at heart and love to play with children. Even though I got paid for a lot of the babysitting I did, I didn't just see taking care of kids as just a job. I saw it as a chance to be a part of a child's life, which is a huge opportunity in my mind. Extending myself in this way also gave me an opportunity to get to know kids better. I learned a range of mothering skills from making a bottle and changing diapers to dealing with surly teenagers. This was an extremely fulfilling experience that helped to lessen some of the pain of not being able to conceive myself. In a way, it was a very fun way to experience mothering, because, at the end of the day, I could always go home to my own place. It wasn't the total immersion version that many mothers are thrown into.

When we first started going to church with my sister, I noticed that she would buy boring things for the kids to entertain themselves with, and so I started packing my bag with really fun things like stickers and fun books and quiet toys to help try and entertain the kids. My niece and nephew always loved sitting with me because of all the stuff in my bag. People started calling it my "Mary Poppins bag." I don't always end up sitting beside my sister at church now as her children are older, and she doesn't need as much help with them anymore, but I always bring my Mary Poppins bag because there have been so many times when I've sat beside a family with kids who are having a hard time in church and who I've been able to help and connect with. I love kids because they keep me young and let me be the big kid I really am. Kids bring so much joy into my life.

And after all of that time and all of those experiences, the craziest thing has happened . . . I'm three months pregnant!
—Mia

No matter how we invite women into our lives, my hope is that we all continue on in the grand tradition of using allomothers for the benefit of ourselves, our children, and the allomothers as well. We can find these women in our extended families and our communities—women who want to be adopted just as much as you want to adopt them. Finding those grandmas, aunties, and big sisters can be a huge help and relief to moms, as well as a source of joy and belonging for those allomothers who are embraced as cherished villagers.

# ENDNOTES

1.  Hrdy, *Mothers and Others*

# CHAPTER 11

# Give and Take

As I look back, I realize I could have asked for more help during my last pregnancy and the following year. Asking for help, particularly when you aren't in a position to give back, is a hard thing to do. Taking without giving back is never an ideal scenario, but when you are in a particularly tough spot, you may not have the ability to give back. Sometimes, all you can do is bank your gratitude for a time when you can generously pay it forward.

Admittedly, during my last pregnancy, simply banking my gratitude felt uncomfortable. That was not the only problem—I had been in the mud for so long I didn't really even know what to ask for. It's sometimes hard to come up with a response when people say, "If there's anything I can do to help out, just let me know," when you don't even know what would help.

## Accepting Help

I wish I would have asked for and accepted more help (from my church community, especially). I didn't because I didn't know those women very well, and I felt uncomfortable asking for help when I had not ever given anything to them. With the people who offered help, I wish I would have invited them over and asked them to help me clean my kitchen or wash my bed sheets—something that would have welcomed freshness into my home. Or I wish I would have asked them to come over to hold my baby while I took a shower and perhaps taken a few minutes to exercise, meditate, or pray. Someone could also have helped me make freezer meals so that future dinners were handy and nutritious. I would have loved someone lip syncing and dancing to Olivia Newton John's "Xanadu" in my living room, because that kind of stuff can put a smile on my face for days.

Reaching out for extra help would have helped me practically, but now I realize, even more importantly, I would have had more opportunity to connect with those who offered help. And I would have had an increased confidence in the support that was around me. Perception of support is even more important than the actual support received in combating postpartum depression; new moms need to believe that they are a part of a support network that will catch them if they fall.

Here's a story from a single mother who had to learn to ask for help:

> When I moved to Edmonton, I only knew a few people, and since I was in night class twice a week, I relied on the relatives I had there to look after my son, Jaren, those nights. One night it was my aunt, whom we knew quite well. The other night it was my dad's cousin's wife, Michelle. I had never met Michelle before we moved, but I will never forget how kind she was to me. Michelle is an enthusiastic mom! She came to our place once a week for three and a half months to babysit my son even though she had four of her own kids at home. She always played with Jaren and had fun little gifts for him.
>
> She and her family were there for me the whole three years I was in university! They would watch him if I needed to study on a weekend afternoon or if I wanted to go out at night with some friends. No doubt the hardest part about being a single mom is that you can't leave your house easily. No running out quickly for some groceries or going for a walk or run for exercise. You have to do all those things while the child is at school or day care or else hire a babysitter, which really adds up when you are also the only source of income. Arranging babysitters for my son gave me a countless amount of stomach aches. I had to debate whether I could afford to pay someone. How would I get the babysitter

home once my son was asleep—should I just wake him up to drive him? Could I ask a relative or, in asking them, was I taking advantage of them? I constantly worried that I was asking too much of the people around me.

But, not one mother ever made me feel uncomfortable asking them. They always welcomed my son, and many went out of their way to help me out. It was a real blessing in my life to have so many good mothers that supported me in Edmonton. And their support wasn't just practical; it was emotional, too.

My neighbor Laurel was another mom who took my son every Wednesday afternoon for a full school year, despite the fact that she would then sometimes have to be late picking up her own son from school. Laurel taught me how it's possible to form a community while living in a huge city. Her kindness to neighbors and friends warms my heart every time I think of her.

Jodine lived down the street from us, and they had a mixed family of four kids at home, plus two grown ones with two grandkids thrown in that were always coming and going from their place. Yet they took Jaren whenever they could, and one of their sons babysat Jaren every Monday after school while I worked. Jodine taught me to relax a little more as a mom; I learned the value of flexibility from her.

Being a single mom forces you to rely on others, and because I have been on my own I can appreciate the saying, "It takes a village to raise a child." I can only do so much, and, since I don't have a partner to rely on, I have had to look for numerous other sources. I think in a way all these other sources will benefit my son in the long run because, just as it has exposed me to new and wonderful people, it has exposed him to them as well.

I have learned how self-involved we can be when we get busy with our lives, and that it's so easy to miss that the person sitting next to you might need help. For eight years now, I have been one of those people who constantly needs support! It's a strange feeling and a strange thing to admit because, prior to having my son, I considered myself to be a pretty independent person. Being a mom keeps us humble. It's an impossible job to do alone, and I imagine that even having a partner isn't enough support because you still need time with them to nourish that relationship. I love the concept of "pay it forward." I have had help from so many other moms that I no longer live close to, but I hope to return their kindness by offering to help new moms that I meet along my life's journey. The offer of help from another mom, who can understand what you are going through, is something I hope all moms have a chance to have. It's something all moms need.

—Elisha

## Boundaries

Part of reaching out for help includes asking others to accept a "no" when you need to give one. It is also just as important to graciously accept a "no" when someone else needs to give you one. Some women sail through pregnancy and may not realize the challenges you are facing, and the same is true of the first year of motherhood. There are things I had to say no to after my third was born that I never would have after my first or second. Other people can't read your mind, and they don't know what is happening in your life.

Remember that your sanity is so very important—don't lose it because you are afraid of letting other people down.

The other weekend my sister-in-law was visiting me with her one-year-old, who was adjusting to a new place and a new routine. They had been busy visiting family prior to stopping at my house, and her son was not sleeping well. She was exhausted. We woke up one morning and went to the park. I pitched the idea of going swimming with the kids after naps that afternoon before meeting up for supper with the rest of the family. She explained that she was a one-activity-per-day kind of a gal at that moment and that she just needed to take the rest of the day kind of slow. Good for her for saying no, thank you! I appreciated her honesty, because then I didn't have to worry about her quietly resenting me for dragging her exhausted behind all over the city when what she really needed was just rest.

Establishing boundaries has been something I have really had to work on myself. Boundaries are an essential part of good working relationships, but it's sometimes not so easy to figure out.

One day, a friend of mine asked if I could take her kids for a couple of hours. I always want to help this friend out whenever I can, because she has helped me out in a pinch many times. We have an extremely good working relationship as well as a valued friendship. That particular day, though, I had a doctor's appointment and had to pick up my son from school, and it would have been obvious to anyone looking at my schedule that it just wasn't going to work. My mistake was that I started explaining my schedule, but I didn't do a very good job of it. I wasn't able to explain all the reasons why it wouldn't work, and, because there was a hint of desperation in her voice, I, against good sense, agreed to take her kids.

It didn't work out, and I ended up missing my son's school pick-up from the bus stop. Since I have an arrangement with the day care he gets dropped off in front of, he ended up going into the day care instead of home. I had to pay the day care $20.00 to take care of my son, because I was looking after someone else's kids.

Yeah, I have boundary issues. I know my friend well enough to know she would never have expected me to take her kids if she knew the inconvenience it caused, and I didn't tell her about the $20.00 because I didn't want her to feel bad about it, but this was a red flag for me. I realized that I needed to learn the art of boundary creation.

I have since learned that I can't always explain my schedule to someone else; sometimes I forget important things that need to get done but have a nagging feeling in the back of my mind that I know I have something going on. Learning to write down my to-do items has helped me know when and where I can give to others, but until I perfect that skill, I find it best to simply offer a kind but firm no when I'm feeling tempted to offer something I don't have the ability to give. Phrases like "I'm sorry, I have stuff going on all day that day," or "Rats, I wish that could work. My kids really love playing with your kids, but that time doesn't work for us." Keeping it vague and kind (but still firm) allows you to keep it honest. At the same time, it does not invite those who may struggle with respecting boundaries to feel like figuring out your schedule is an open brainstorming session.

If you struggle with respecting other people's boundaries, perhaps take some time to discover why that is and look for strategies that can help you be at peace with respecting other people's space and their decisions. It's good and even important to ask for help, but it's also equally important to respectfully accept a no if the person you are requesting help from is not in a position to give. It is very probable that any fellow mama you are asking help from is also feeling overwhelmed, and it's possible that she may be in desperate need of help at that moment as well.

Certainly, there will be times when you have nothing to give, when all you can do is take, but whenever possible, it is best to find balance A true friendship is a give-and-take thing. Over time, throughout the seasons of imbalance, a healthy friendship should balance out. If you are always giving or always taking, reevaluate how you engage in your relationships. Perhaps, to find a better balance, you may need to initate a conversation to build stronger boundaries.

Take time and consideration before you engage in these important conversations. Often, timing is essential; try to find a time when your friend can handle processing some difficult emotions and is in a place where she has the resources to make some changes. The right time is rarely the point when your anger finally boils over. You have to listen and acknowledge your anger, but you don't have to let it be your boss, and it shouldn't be out of control when you start the conversation. My advice: however hurt, taken advantage of, or distanced you may be feeling toward someone else, always be the kindest version of yourself. If you need to have an emotional talk with someone, never forget to bring your humility and compassion along for the ride. Feeling hurt is part of the experience of being vulnerable enough to connect. Be hurt—but leave the anger at home.

# A String and a Knife

Samuel Butler, a nineteenth century English writer, wrote a small essay entitled "Joining and Disjoining." He explains that, in stumbling upon some of his old scribbles, he found these words: "All things are either of the nature of a piece of string or a knife. That is, they are either for bringing and keeping things together, or for sending and keeping them apart."

He remarked on his earlier thought and then went on to add some depth. He explained that a train is something that brings people together, but it is also something that sends them apart. A farmer's hedge is also "both for joining things (as a flock of sheep) and for disjoining (as for keeping the sheep from getting into corn)."[1] He concludes:

> A piece of string is a thing that, in the main makes for togetheriness; whereas a knife is, in the main, a thing that makes for splitty-uppiness; still, there is an odour of togetherness hanging about a knife also, for it tends to bring potatoes into a man's stomach.

> In high philosophy one should never look at a knife without considering it also as a piece of string, nor at a piece of string without considering it also as a knife.[2]

His insight is also true for setting boundaries. A boundary can seem like its purpose is disjoining, but the right boundary can actually facilitate togetherness. Good fences really do make good neighbors.

Being integrated with other moms means learning not just how to give, but also how to receive, and how to build your fences in just the right places. This is a process that might feel uncomfortable to begin, but will be less difficult if you can approach the effort with generosity, gratitude, and humility. Leaning on others during hard times can be rough on your pride, but it can also grow your heart in a big way. Accepting service is an opportunity to see some golden-mama heroes in action. It is a chance to see powerful examples of how you can, in turn, effectively reach out to others.

# ENDNOTES

1.  Samuel Butler, "Joining and Disjoining," *Literature in English*, ed. W. H. New and W. E. Messenger (Scarborough, Ontario: Prentice Hall Canada, 1993), 1088–1089.

2.  Ibid.

# CHAPTER 12

# Strong Villages Are Built on Solid Emotional Foundations

There is an old story that one day, a man died and was ushered into the afterlife. His guide showed him to a room where there was a large feast set on a table, with many other people seated at the table. Each person's hands, which held chopsticks, were tied to the person's next to them. Everyone was eagerly trying to feed themselves, and as they fought against those whose hands their hands were tied to, they were all left miserable and hungry. The guide said to the man, "This is hell." He then ushered the man to a room next door, which was identical to the first. All the people were seated around a delicious feast, chopsticks in hand. Again, each person's hands were tied to his or her neighbor's; however, in that room everyone was using their chopsticks to feed one another. All were being fed, all were happy. The guide said to the man, "This is heaven."

When I was in Taiwan, whenever I would eat with locals, they would always be gracious and offer me a fork. However, I was determined to pick up the chopsticks and become as proficient with them as the Taiwanese. Even the children deftly used them; surely I could. I was clumsy with them in the beginning, and more than once I would be eating one rice kernel at a time, but I got better—even good. Similarly, if you have the desire to be more inclusive, collective, and loving, you might at first be clumsy and make a bit of a mess, but the more you work at it, the better you'll get.

I have been clumsy with others most of my life, but I believe I can improve there. I want that heaven. I want to be a part of that great, joyful feast. So here

I am, with rice on the floor, occasionally dropping tofu in someone else's lap, trying my best to feed the people at my table. None of us are perfect. We all make mistakes in our attempts to love each other, and it may just be for the best, so that we can authentically pull out a large dose of grace when we are the ones who get tofu dumped in our laps.

As we go about trying our best to feed each other (often awkwardly), we can become more proficient in caring for others by understanding and strengthening our emotional selves. Building relationships in your village, those that will be strong enough to support you throughout life, requires mastering the art of loving others and yourself. God can help you, the mystic in training, learn these skills as he whispers truth to your heart and sends teachers to cross your path.

## Everyone is a Little Broken

A great step toward becoming more loving is to develop a willingness to be vulnerable. I think Brené Brown, author of *The Gifts of Imperfection*, is a teacher who was sent my way at just the right time. She writes, "We cultivate love when we allow our most vulnerable and powerful selves to be deeply seen and known."[1]

One mother I interviewed shared how her mother's willingness to admit mistakes and withhold judgment both emboldened her and allowed them to have a close relationship.

> My mother has always been open with me about her imperfections. She allowed me to see them, to see her struggles with them, as well as her triumphs. When she made mistakes mothering me, she would come and apologize (even if we'd had an emotional argument about it first). I know she struggles to accept the good things within herself, and yet she has always accepted me. Her acceptance of my goals, my decisions, and my aspirations has allowed me to pursue them. Her belief that I could accomplish all of those, if that's what I wanted, made them attainable.
>
> —Denise

Denise's mother set the example of being open and vulnerable with her family, empowering Denise to develop and accomplish great things. But being vulnerable is not easy for many reasons. I personally hate feeling vulnerable—I have always hated it. Being vulnerable means taking chances with your heart. It is risking being really seen by those in your life, which can be an intimidating endeavor. It is definitely easier to hide behind a nice outfit, a plate of cupcakes, or some outer show of strength and ability than to bring our real selves to the table. But I have found over and over that when I offer my most authentic self to those around me, the risk has, more often than not, paid off in terms of a richer connection and comfort with others.

Brown states, "I think we should be born with a warning label similar to the ones that come on cigarette packages: Caution: If you trade in your authenticity for safety, you may experience the following: anxiety, depression, eating disorders, addiction, rage, blame, resentment, and inexplicable grief."[2]

Connection requires authenticity. Authenticity requires honesty. Being dishonest with yourself and others—even if practiced in slight and seemingly harmless shades—will poison the love in your life.

I especially find this to be true when it comes to being honest about my own shortcomings and weaknesses. Being upfront with myself and others about the fact that I am a work in progress makes apologies so much easier when I happen to drop that sticky piece of tofu. I don't pretend that remembering birthdays isn't as hard as climbing Everest for me—I even forgot my *own* birthday one year. I let my friends know that they shouldn't try to lend me things because I don't take care of anyone's stuff very well—mine included. If I'm being honest with myself, I know that there's a good chance I'll either lose whatever they lend me or simply forget to ever return it. In admitting these shortcomings, among others, I establish with my friends a connection and an authenticity that invites them to do the same. We are better friends because of it, and we see each other for the beautiful works in progress that we are.

We are *all* a little broken.

We *all* make mistakes.

We are *all* works in progress.

It's natural to feel a little uncomfortable with the vulnerability that accompanies admitting our weaknesses to ourselves and to others. But this kind of beautiful honesty opens the door for our fellow villagers to offer their most authentic and honest selves to us as well. This is an essential part of laying a strong emotional foundation for your village.

## Facing the Hand You've Been Dealt

I found honesty to be a sometimes annoying but ultimately helpful companion during my climb out of the pit of postpartum depression. Embracing honesty helped me face choices I was making in my life that were holding me back from being happy. Brown rightly observes, "We cannot selectively numb emotions. When we numb the painful emotions, we also numb the positive emotions."[3]

Reading Brown's wise words was a lightbulb moment in my life. I experienced so much physical and emotional pain throughout my last pregnancy and the following postpartum period that I retreated, I ran, I hid, and I tried my very best to shut out the world that for me had become a nightmare. My favorite hiding place was in food. It took awhile for me to realize that I was consistently using food in a really damaging way. I was desperately trying to numb my painful emotions. Food seemed like a relatively safe place to hide, but in no way did it bring joy or connection to my life. I was numbing not only the bad and the ugly but also the good. It took time, courage, honesty, and kindness to myself to finally peek my head out into the world again.

We all use life's pleasures—food, shopping, social media, entertainment, and countless others—to brighten our lives at times, and when done in moderate amounts, I think that's a good thing. It gets messy when they become the thing we consistently turn to for solace or comfort. When you ignore your emotional self, you are perfectly aligned to pick up any of those things Brown listed: "anxiety, depression, eating disorders, addiction, rage, blame, resentment, and inexplicable grief."

There are different ways to figure yourself out emotionally: books, therapists, yoga, support groups. You have to find what works best for you as you work toward building a strong emotional foundation.

My family doctor thought I would benefit from a little visit with the friendly old psychiatrist, as he knew I had been diagnosed with ADHD decades earlier but had not sought any professional help. For most of my life, I had ignored the diagnosis and was able to cope by creating a life for myself that worked with the inherent wiring of someone with ADHD. When I met with the psychiatrist, who was a specialist in adult ADHD, my mind was blown. I began to see how so much of the tension in my life was related to my brain chemistry.

I also learned that most women with ADHD don't find themselves in front of a psychiatrist until they have kids, because that's often when things really start to fall apart for us. A few of our weaknesses are focus, organization, time management, and impulsivity. As a stay-at-home mom, my entire job is to keep the family organized, keep time as I drum out our family's schedule, and provide a consistent, calm life for my children. In other words: Mission *Impossible*. Basically, my job description is a list of every one of my weaknesses.

Problems that arise from not understanding or giving proper attention to our mental and emotional well-being can result in severe stress. One of the questions I was asked at my evaluation was if I suffered from neck or back pain or headaches, because consistent stress can lead to physical pain. I suffered from all of them.

Understanding this was a crucial step for me to get to the truth of who I really am and how I relate with my family and my community. This recognition helped me realize exactly what was going on that day when I emerged from our computer room and informed my husband that I was going to buy a tent trailer and take off with the kids for the entire summer, aimlessly traveling all over the United States. I enthusiastically told him, "This is such a great idea! You might get a call from me in two weeks: 'Hey! I'm in New Orleans, and it's so cool here. You should hop on a plane and come visit us.'" He responded with an understandably nervous look on his face.

Now that I know myself better, I understand there are other options available to help me cope with life that don't include becoming a nomad (which is all I've ever really wanted). This information is also helpful for my husband, who now understands that when I say things like that, I'm not rejecting him; I am just trying to cope with the stress in my life, and my impulsivity often chimes in during my attempts at problem solving.

Many women struggle with anxiety, mood, eating, or personality disorders and various other mental illnesses. All of these disorders can be significant roadblocks in your attempts at developing and maintaining friendships. It's important to understand your own fundamental wiring in order to make the most of whatever wiring you happen to be stuck with.

Information is power. Truth is liberating.

The more information and truth you can get your hands on, the easier connecting with others will become. I'd like to give a big shout-out to good, quality mental health professionals who can help us figure ourselves out, so we can strengthen our emotional foundations.

## Time For a Cage Remodel?

Another thing I realized along my journey inward and upward is that it is very common for people who feel lonely and disconnected to develop addictions. Understandably, it's sometimes easier to pull off a Houdini-inspired disappearing act than to stay present during a painful time in your life. In the 1970s, Bruce K. Alexander, PhD, Professor Emeritus of Simon Fraser University, along with some of his colleagues, wanted to look more closely at the nature of addiction and performed an experiment that changed the way people view addiction.

They altered an experiment done the previous decade, during which researchers put a rat in a cage with two sources of water: one with pure water and another with cocaine-laced water. The researchers in this first experiment found that the rat ignored the pure water and eventually killed itself by overdosing on the cocaine-laced water. This led researchers to believe that the drug was the obvious cause of the rat's addiction and eventual death.

In Alexander's experiment, Alexander and his team similarly offered their rats both the pure water and the cocaine-laced water, but they changed one variable: the cage. They put the rats in what they called "Rat Park." Rat Park was a little heaven for rats. Rather than placing the rat alone in a tiny cage, they placed it in a large enclosed space that had platforms for climbing, tin cans for hiding, wood chips for strewing around, and running wheels for exercise. This rat mansion also had lots of other rats, male and female, so the rats could exist in an environment similar to their natural one, where they live as highly social, sexual, and industrious creatures.

The second experiment yielded significantly different results from the first. The rats living in Rat Park, unlike the isolated ones, had little to no interest in the cocaine-laced water and generally stayed away from it. They, in fact, thrived in Rat Park. This led the researchers to believe that it was not the drug that was the problem—*it was the cage.*[4]

Viewing addiction in this way has been extremely enlightening as I work on my own emotional health. It's common for people with ADHD to develop addictions, and I could see that my relationship with food was getting a little too serious . . . I was close to going ring shopping with it.

Recovering addicts are extraordinary people. For many addicts, the price they have to pay if they do not figure themselves out and work to overcome the addiction is enormous. Their marriages, jobs, and families are often on the line. Many addicts are literally fighting for their lives. It is this desperation that drives many addicts to dedicate themselves to the effort of emotional, spiritual, and physical wellness. Recovering addicts are some of the wisest and most emotionally healthy people I have ever met. They are so wise because they have had to untangle themselves from the emotional, mental, physical, and spiritual complications of having an addiction. They have had to look at their own cages and figure out what was missing from them. So often addicts find that what they are trying to replace with their drug of choice is some quality companionship in their own little Rat Parks.

There is an undeniable tie between addiction and human connection, and Roger Stark, an addictions counselor, had this to say concerning the correlation:

> Forming an addiction is often an effort to replace the benefits that
> human relationships were intended to give us, which we feel are

missing in our lives. We try to harvest from our addiction the nurturing and comfort that should come from developing and maintaining healthy relationships.

Addiction is more than a behavior. Addiction starts with an emotional attachment, or relationship if you will. An emotional bond is formed to alcohol, prescription drugs, food, gambling, etc., that becomes a compulsive attachment. He or she cannot do without it. The object of the addiction becomes the best friend, lover, and the demon that will destroy the addict.[5]

After my visit to the doctor, I timidly started going to OA (Overeaters Anonymous) meetings to deal with my Godzilla-in-Candyland issue. Food had become my worst best friend. It was what I consistently turned to when I felt trapped and alone; it kept me company in the same way a diseased bat might offer company to an isolated prisoner of war. Whenever an uncomfortable feeling came my way, I felt so ill-equipped to cope that I chose to put food in the spotlight, so I didn't have to deal with anything else. Sometimes declaring war on yourself is an easy way to distract yourself from pressing domestic affairs.

I found a great online support group called In The Rooms (https://www.intherooms.com/). You can participate in video meetings for various types of addictions on the website. That is where I found my sponsor, whom I love dearly. It is also where I met many others who regularly showed up for the meetings and shared their truth with me.

The Twelve Steps developed by William Griffith Wilson (Bill W.) in 1938 are still used today and are absolute *magic*. They can be applied to any type of addiction and are so broadly useful, because at their core, they help to facilitate connection with others through an intimate connection with a higher power. They help you to make your own Rat Park as rich as it can be. I want to share them here.

1.     We admitted we were powerless over [our addiction]—that our lives had become unmanageable.

2.     [We] came to believe that a Power greater than ourselves could restore us to sanity.

3.     [We] made a decision to turn our will and our lives over to the care of God *as we understood Him.*

4.     [We] made a searching and fearless moral inventory of ourselves.

5.     [We] admitted to God, to ourselves, and to another human being the exact nature of our wrongs.

6.     [We] were entirely ready to have God remove all these defects of character.

7.     [We] humbly asked Him to remove our shortcomings.

8.     [We] made a list of all persons we had harmed, and became willing to make amends to them all.

9.     [We] made direct amends to such people wherever possible, except when to do so would injure them or others.

10.    [We] continued to take personal inventory and when we were wrong promptly admitted it.

11.    [We] sought through prayer and meditation to improve our conscious contact with God, *as we understood Him,* praying only for knowledge of His will for us and the power to carry that out.

12.    Having had a spiritual awakening as the result of these Steps, we tried to carry this message to [other addicts], and to practice these principles in all our affairs.

When you go through the Twelve Steps, you really are starting out a caterpillar and ending up a butterfly. It is major renovation work, but in the end, it offers a beautiful home built on a solid foundation. The basis of any 12-step program is the belief that we need both a higher power and a community of support to do what we could never do by ourselves. It is leaving your island to go to the mainland. For me, it has been the perfect place to be tutored in how to connect to God, myself, and others in emotionally healthy and productive ways.

The 12-step meetings are very special gatherings. They offer a space for people to come out of hiding and admit the worst of the worst. To tell your darkest tales, your craziest crazy. The beautiful thing is that everyone else seems to have the same stories. In the middle of sharing some moment of shame and regret, it can be both a surprise and a relief to see heads nod with sad smiles of recognition. OA helped me feel how understanding and empathy can be powerfully healing and transformative. It also reinforced my belief that sharing our stories is important. We need to tell them, and other people need to hear them.

One of the most impactful ways OA helped me clean up some darkness in my life and strengthen my connection with others was working through steps four and nine: making a fearless, investigative moral inventory of myself and making amends. I started by picking up the phone and offering some apologies. It was a frightening and unappealing idea at first. Despite how uncomfortable it sounds, I had one of the most satisfying conversations of my entire life when I called one of my family members. I started with a humble, "Hey, remember that time when . . . ? I'm just so sorry I acted poorly then. I realize now that I have a lot to work on, and I really love you and want you to know how sorry I am that I can be so clumsy with you at times." As satisfying as that sorry was to give, it was even more satisfying to hear the apology accepted wholeheartedly with a reciprocal offering of, "Oh, man, I know I'm not perfect either, relationships can be tough to maneuver. I'm sorry, too."

That phone call was chopstick heaven. It melted my ego in the most beautiful way. I was hooked. I couldn't stop saying sorry to people after that, because every sorry I offered, big or small, made me feel lighter and lighter. Even writing this now, I can think of a few more people I could offer an apology to. The idea still makes me feel nervous, but I know now the courage required is worth it.

If you are feeling lonely, a productive question to ask yourself is: Is there something in my life that I am substituting for real connections with others? TV? Food? Work? Drugs? Alcohol? Sex? What I found in those OA meetings was a gorgeous and inspiring outpouring of honesty, humility, faith, and love from those who came to share and heal. And together, we worked to overcome unhealthy addictions. It's a place where people thank you for allowing them the opportunity to be of service to you. It is a place where people who are desperate for a change find hope and miracles as they learn to work with their higher power. I have been consistently amazed by the quality of connections within the 12-step programs and their beautifully rigorous practice of humility. Through this transformative experience, I have learned so much about how my emotional health has an enormous impact on the quality of my relationships.

Sometimes there are dysfunctions within us that block our ability to connect with others. Do we know how to handle our anger? Our insecurities? Our fears? What is our emotional relationship with ourselves? Are we ashamed, scared, or mean to ourselves? Ultimately, the key to connecting to a meaningful community is, with God's help, to connect to yourself, be in touch with yourself—to "know thyself." Be kind in this endeavor, and create a loving relationship with yourself first.

Having a satisfying community is more intimate than I first realized, because it is possible to be completely surrounded by people and yet still feel excruciatingly alone inside. As you turn your life over to your higher power, you will be guided in assembling your community in ways that bring goodness, wisdom, and love into your life.

# ENDNOTES

1.  Brené Brown, *The Gifts of Imperfection* (Center City, MN: Hazelden, 2010), 26.

2.  Ibid., 53.

3.  Ibid., 70.

4.  Bruce K. Alexander, "Addiction: The View from Rat Park (2010)," Bruce K. Alexander's official website, http://www.brucekalexander.com/articles-speeches/rat-park/148-addiction-the-view-from-rat-park.

5.  Roger Stark, *The Waterfall Concept: A Blueprint for Addiction Recovery* (Brush Prairie, WA: Silver Star Publishing, 2010).

# CHAPTER 13

# Identify the Enemies of Your Village

A s you learn to become kinder to yourself, you'll find it will become easier to offer that kindness to others as well. Shame, ego, and judgment are all common enemies of the village, and these enemies can keep many of us from finding community.

## Shame

Shaming others is a pretty obvious way to obliterate your connection with them. Shaming yourself can be just as troublesome for your relationships, but is sometimes not as obvious.

Shame is the antithesis of freedom.

Shame is isolating and debilitating.

Shame says, "Hide yourself."

Guess how many friends you can make if you are hiding? Unless you are playing a game of hide and seek together, hiding is not likely to help you out in the loneliness department. Shame is an easy enough trap to fall into, but it is most certainly counterproductive.

When I was going through Basic Military Training, I recall a day when our section was to go through a series of evaluations. The two I remember most distinctly were the drill evaluation and the timed obstacle course. Drill is when the recruits gather onto a drill deck and practice different maneuvers with their rifles. It's kind of like synchronized swimming, but on dry land—and with guns.

Our master corporal was a fierce and intimidating man who, despite all of his finely honed dramatic terror, was deeply respected by everyone. We had been practicing drill for weeks with the master corporal, and when it was time for us to show our stuff, we choked. We weren't as tight as we knew we could be, and as a group, we were all extremely disappointed in our performance.

It's difficult to convey the emotion of this failure here because drill may not seem that important to a civilian onlooker, but during Basic Military Training, you are conditioned to believe that every single thing you do is life or death. Even a seemingly simple act, like forgetting to do up one of your buttons, could mean a hellish afternoon of push-ups and marching for your entire section. We were trained to believe that everything mattered, and we were devastated when we blew it.

Our master corporal came to talk to us after the evaluation, and we all thought, *Here it comes. Brace for impact.* But there was no impact. He came up to us with positivity and strength, and he told us that he knew how disappointed we all were but that we had to let our disappointment go. Our lament was dead weight—we had an obstacle course next, and if we dragged our recent failure with us through the obstacle course, we would fail that, too. His message: don't wallow in your failures or your mistakes, because that just weakens you for the important tasks that lie ahead of you.

I gained similar insight from a friend of mine who has learned how to throw her shame in the trash.

> I think that I was isolated partly because we had just moved to a new city but also because I, personally, was not in a good place. I wasn't happy, and I certainly wasn't healthy. I think that shame certainly played a part in that. After Amy was born, it seemed that my friends and I weren't in the same place anymore. Becoming a mother derails your entire social construct. At times, it can feel as though you don't have anything to offer anyone else.
>
> Before I had Amy, I was able to make plans on the fly. After she was born, I spent so much time just with her, and then, when I really

needed to have adult interaction, I had nobody because I hadn't set that up for myself. I felt like, in a way, I wasn't even worthy of having fun, active friends because I was so tied down to my baby. Once I started doing Cycling Mamas and had a regular commitment to do something for myself and to be active, the way I thought about other people changed; joining the Cycling Mamas was the start of a really long period of change. I'm still evolving. I understand now that to make friends I have to intentionally create opportunities, in addition to doing my job and taking care of my family. I would say that I have to be very conscious about not slipping back into my old patterns of hiding away and isolating myself.

There is truth to the idea out there that positive words and thoughts are good for you and will make you stronger—that they can even make you physically stronger. Conversely, things that are negative will make you weaker and suck the life out of you. Shame is the lowest of all the negative things you can feel—shame is the lowest vibration. I've been very intent on eliminating shame from my life, because if there is something that makes me weaker and more powerless, I want to avoid it.

Being able to let go of shame was largely a by-product of growing up and coming into my own. As I did that, it was easier for me to let go of what other people thought of me or were expecting of me. I used to get caught up in trying to please everyone around me. When I didn't live up to others' expectations, I would feel bad about myself and guilty for falling short, which made isolating myself more tempting.

But as I became active, I was better equipped to conquer the temptation. You can't become stronger physically without also becoming stronger emotionally. Particularly as a mother, deciding to become more active was a first step to claiming my own value and worth, and that liberated me from shame.

—Melinda

Shame does nothing but hold us back from bringing our full light and energy to our future selves and to those around us. Our shame lessens when we let go of the idea of perfection and learn to embrace all that we are. In the wise words of Elizabeth Gilbert: "My life seems happiest . . . when I just surrender to the madness, and *embrace the glorious mess that I am* . . . and also when I embrace the glorious mess that everyone else is, and the glorious mess of the world itself."

No one is perfect. Everyone is a little bit broken, and there is no shame in this—only opportunity. Don't be afraid to admit your mistakes, say you're sorry as often as you can, and if you haven't yet, confess to someone you trust that really awful thing you did that one time. Shining a light on all your darkness magically makes the darkness disappear and will help you to develop beautifully honest relationships with others.

# Ego

When I was a teenager, someone told me that whenever you are talking with someone, your objective should not be to make that person feel good about you. Your objective should be to make that person feel good about themselves. It was a revolutionary thought for me, because as I teenager, I was very unsure about myself in so many ways. I often thought I had to be pitching myself to others. But people hate being pitched to. What I think is interesting about that is that I wasn't trying to big myself up to others because I thought I was better than anyone else; I was doing it because I felt inadequate. Both feeling superior to others and feeling inferior to others sets you up for failure when it comes to connecting. Both of those feelings are born of the ego—that place that judges, compares, worships heroes, or denigrates.

We need to be aware of how we view the world. Ego spectacles and soul spectacles will give you two different worldviews. View the world through your ego spectacles and you will see yourself in a lineup, starting from the most successful to the least. Since success is such an unstable construct, if you only ever wear your ego spectacles, you will constantly be in flux in terms of how valuable you feel. Wearing ego spectacles around town means you are in constant competition with everyone around you, because that lineup is all you see.

Soul spectacles, on the other hand, offer a different perspective. Put your soul spectacles on and you will see everyone holding hands in a circle rather than elbowing each other in a line. They will allow you to see that every single soul you come into contact with has the same grand significance as you do. You will see everyone brilliantly lit up with the divinity they bring to this earth when they are born.

You will also be able to feel the strange comfort that can come when you contemplate how small we all are in comparison to the endless galaxies beyond ourselves. With our soul spectacles, we are both emboldened and humbled at the same time and in the same way as everyone else. The view soul spectacles offer will not change if you get fired from your job or if your kids all end up in prison or if by some cruel twist of fate you begin growing a third ear in the middle of your face. With soul spectacles on, it will be so much easier for you to listen more than you talk. It will be easier to be generous with others without expecting anything in return. Looking through your soul spectacles, it is easier for you to speak to everyone as though they were your equal—because you clearly see that they are.

I highly recommend everyone picking up a pair of soul spectacles. They are worth any ego sacrifice required and will definitely help you find some soul sisters to walk through life with.

## Judgment

Motherhood these days is wrought with insecurity. It's hard to feel like you're doing it right, and mistakes are easy to make. An almost fail-proof method of distancing yourself from others is to judge them. This is an especially easy mistake to make when you're just starting your mothering career. It's so easy to look at another mom and think, *I would never do that. What is she thinking? Doesn't she know that she should never raise her voice at her child? Lucky for my future kids, I will only speak in a Mary Poppins, practically-perfect-in-every-way voice (throwing in the occasional show tune to balance my calm discipline with just the right amount of fun).*

It's easy to be impatient with other people's shortcomings, especially if your memory takes a shifty little holiday when pressed to remember all the times in your own life when you've made solidly bad choices. The truth is that we can never really know what's going on in someone else's life—ever. Stephen Covey relates an experience in his book *The 7 Habits of Highly Effective People*.

> I remember a mini-paradigm shift I experienced one Sunday morn-ing on a subway in New York. People were sitting quietly—some reading newspapers, some lost in thought, some resting with their eyes closed. It was a calm, peaceful scene. Then suddenly, a man and his children entered the subway car. The children were so loud and rambunctious that instantly the whole climate changed.
>
> The man sat down next to me and closed his eyes, apparently oblivious to the situation. The children were yelling back and forth, throwing things, even grabbing people's papers. It was very disturb-ing. And yet, the man sitting next to me did nothing.
>
> It was difficult not to feel irritated. I could not believe that he could be so insensitive to let his children run wild like that and do noth-ing about it, taking no responsibility at all. It was easy to see that everyone else on the subway felt irritated, too. So finally, with what I felt was unusual patience and restraint, I turned to him and said, "Sir, your children are really disturbing a lot of people. I wonder if you couldn't control them a little more?"
>
> The man lifted his gaze as if to come to a consciousness of the situation for the first time and said softly, "Oh, you're right. I guess I should do something about it. We just came from the hospital where their mother died about an hour ago. I don't know what to think, and I guess they don't know how to handle it either."[1]

It's easy to make quick judgments about others; however, they are most often useless, unhelpful, and incorrect—regardless of how clever or right you think you are. There is also the temptation sometimes to feel like when we *do* know a lot about someone else, that we can then judge them because we have all the information we need to do so. However, people are so complex and often so reluctant to disclose their deepest and darkest that it is most likely that you will never know the whole picture, even with those closest to you. Having faith in my ignorance has helped me feel compassion instead of spite for others many times in my life. It has helped to just keep repeating to myself, "I don't know the backstory. It could really be an incredible backstory."

I've found that if I want to attract a community, the best way to do that is to encourage others, be patient with them, forget the judgment, and most certainly forget about competition. In our insecurities as mothers, it's tempting to make judgments that place ourselves as somehow better than others to soothe an ego that has not been stroked in a very long time, because, let's be honest, motherhood can be brutal on the ego. Feeling your worth as a mother with crazy hair, oatmeal-streaked clothing, and a foggy brain can be challenging.

Here are a couple of great examples of women who were strengthened by others because they were willing to be vulnerable.

> The worst time I ever had was when I took my six-month-old to Philadelphia on my own, and it was one of those sleeping maniac nights. You know, waking every hour, crying and screaming, and you just don't know what to do. After taking him out of his crib, I picked him up, put him back in his bed, and yelled at him. It was so terrible, and I felt so guilty. To calm myself down, I walked out of the room and tried to do some yoga and deep breathing. I was on my own and I needed to restore some sanity.

> Later, still feeling so guilty about it I called my girlfriends, and they just said, "Sandra, my gosh, we have been there so many times. We've locked ourselves in closets, crying because of not knowing what to do with a screaming child that just won't sleep." When they told me that, I didn't feel like the worst mother on the planet anymore. Knowing that other moms struggle as well helps me a lot.
>
> —Sandra

> My husband and I had three children in three and a half years. It has been challenging, to say the least. On top of our regular struggles with young children, we have had to deal with speech delays and learning difficulties in more than one of our children.

My sister-in-law seems to have a different life; her husband is a
doctor, they haven't had financial stress as we have, and her life just
seems . . . very together. I, on the other hand, lose my patience easily.
One day I was talking to my sister-in-law, and when I mentioned my
struggles with my temper and asked how she never seemed to yell
at her kids, she said to me, "Anna, you and your husband have had
to deal with some really hard things." When she said that, I felt so
validated. It meant a lot to me to hear someone else say, "Hey, you're
going through some tough stuff, and you're doing great with the circumstances," instead of passing judgment and making me feel worse.

—Anna

It takes practice to become a nonjudgmental person. And as you become
more nonjudgmental, I think it can be natural to develop a dislike for seeing
others being judgmental. When you get to that place, it may feel like a trick
question on the test of life: Can't we judge those who are so distastefully judgmental? The answer is still no. It is always no. Once you get to a place where
you don't even pass judgment on the judgers, you will probably start seeing
Yoda in a seventh dimension on a regular basis. Good for you.

Perhaps the key is not to step on others to raise yourself, but rather to
humbly accept yourself as an imperfect human being while remembering
your divine worth *and* the divine worth of those you come into contact
with.

Years ago, I felt extremely annoyed by a certain person. I didn't understand her, and I felt consistently rubbed the wrong way by her. Having
been raised to fall on my knees in prayer daily, it was no extraordinary thing
that one day I found myself kneeling down, opening my irritated heart
to God. I wasn't asking for love or charity or anything; I just appreciated
being able to unload my frustrations in prayer, if only to simply be heard.

I started, "This person is so crazy, right? I mean she does this and that and
. . . I mean . . . I'm sure we're on the same page here . . . " And then a moment
of mysticism happened. I felt an almost overwhelming sense of a very large
magnificent love, and I felt God communicate to me, "I love this person *so*
much, C. J. This much and more."

I was astounded by the love and respect that God held for that person—a person who, up until that point, I didn't think very much of. In that moment, I experienced so much more than a simple reminder that God loves everyone. I was given a glimpse of His love, I was allowed to feel a portion of it, and it was a feeling I recall often when I meet someone who frustrates me. Connecting to that unified whole, bound together by love in a spiritual way helped me open my heart to people who I would not eagerly open my heart to.

This work of withholding judgment is largely inside work. If you are silently passing judgment on another and you think you are keeping your disapproval a secret, most likely you're not fooling anyone. People know. They can sense what your heart feels about them.

Biting your tongue is always a good start, but, in order to bring your most authentic self to the table, you'll need to do the honest work of sincerely becoming a more loving and understanding person—not just sounding like one.

Letting go of judgment means practicing forgiveness on a regular basis. As Dieter F. Uchdorft said so beautifully, "Forgiveness connects principles, it connects people. . . . It is the beginning of an honest path, and it is one of our best hopes for a happy family."[2]

Although I've only touched on three enemies of the village, I'm sure there are many more. Alan McGinnis's book, *The Friendship Factor*, is one of many great books I recommend for learning how to strengthen your relationships and improve your patterns of relating with others. McGinnis mentions other enemies of the village, such as not making your relationships a priority, not being able to open up to others, not giving others their space, being dishonest, trying to have too many friends, being controlling or manipulative, withholding words of appreciation and love, and more. It will take time to learn about how to be a good friend, especially if you feel like you may be starting from ground zero, but it is worth the time.

My main point in this chapter is that who you are on the inside is directly correlated to the quality of your community. A powerful way to defend yourself against shame, ego, and judgment is to understand and appreciate the divinely given value in yourself and in every person you come into contact with.

# ENDNOTES

1.    Stephen Covey, *The 7 Habits of Highly Effective People: Powerful Lessons in Personal Change* (New York: Simon & Schuster, 1989), 16.

2.    Dieter F. Uchtdorf, "One Key to a Happy Family." Liahona magazine. (Salt Lake City: The Church of Jesus Christ of Latter-day Saints, 2012). https://www.lds.org/liahona/2012/10/one-key-to-a-happy-family?lang=eng

# CHAPTER 14

# Serve Your Fellow Moms

Service changes people. It refines, purifies, gives a finer perspective, and brings out the best in each one of us. It gets us
looking outward instead of inward. It prompts us to consider
others' needs ahead of our own.
    —Derek Cuthbert

A friend of mine once said to me that every day, she tries to do
something for herself, something for her kids, and something for
her community. One day, that translated into making some baked
goods (which she loved) with her kids (which they loved) and delivering some
of them to neighbors (which they loved). It seemed like a great idea, so I
thought I would try it myself. I think it lasted for a whole day—maybe two.
It's hard work, adding service into your life when you are already a busy, tired,
and overstretched mom.

## On Throwing Your Boomerang

Service, like most things in life, must be approached prudently. There are
times when I have extended myself in service and have felt it enrich my life
and even energize me. Reaching out to others can help put your own challenges into perspective. Service can lighten your own load and can, at times,
not require that much extra effort on your part.

One day, I was at Home Depot trying to pick up some lumber to fix our little deck. I was in a hurry and eager to just get my stuff done. I needed help getting the lumber into my van, and so a young guy was paged to come and help me.

As he was loading my van, I whipped out my phone and started to read. Surprisingly, the young man seemed to want to chat. Seriously—he wanted to chat. He asked me a question I can't even remember, but it was definitely an in-depth "How's it going?" kind of a question. So, I decided to be a little more generous than I wanted to be, and I gave him my full attention. He was a young man stuck in what seemed to him to be a dead-end job. He loved reading and writing poetry and wanted to see the world.

I encouraged him, and we talked about how satisfying writing can be. I told him how much I loved exploring the world. It was a good moment for both of us, and I'm grateful I pulled out a little bit of energy for him. He made me feel like a seasoned, wise, older lady, and he seemed grateful to have had a listening ear. It surprised me that in that hurried moment I was able to connect meaningfully with someone I didn't think I had anything in common with, and that he could fill my emotional tank, helping me realize the value I have in experience and enthusiasm.

However, there have been other times when I have overextended myself, and it has been a disaster for me and my family as I gave away my last drop of energy that really should have been preserved for my little ones, my husband, and myself. So how do you know when service will fill you or when it will sink you? Enter the mystic.

There are so many people who are in need. You will never be able to help them all. Figuring out where to focus your energy is done best by connecting with the divine and seeking inspiration.

When I was young, I got my hands on some contact information for some distant relatives in Romania. Excited to connect, I wrote a letter and sent some money along. Probably no more than five bucks.

The reply was gracious. "I thank you for your letter and also your money, but I am an adult and I have a good job so there is no need to send money, as I am guessing you are a child." I just assumed they were poor because they lived in Romania. To my credit, I was just too young to know better, but the lesson has stayed with me. Giving ignorantly is just a bad idea. The best way to help others is to get to know them well enough that you can avoid things like sending a meal of shrimp pasta to a family with a deadly shellfish allergy.

Allow inspiration to overrule prudence. A friend of mine had to suddenly pack up and move her family to another city. Many people were able to pitch in and help, which was great. One day, I went over and for several hours helped to clean her house and organize her stuff. After I was done, I went home, looked around my own disaster of a house and thought, *What business do I have going over to clean someone else's house when I don't even have time to clean my own?* I thought maybe I had been unwise.

But then my mother-in-law called and told me that she was hiring some cleaners to come to her house to prepare for family coming to town and asked if I would like it if she sent them my way for a few hours. My house has never been cleaner. When you get service right, it's often like a boomerang—you throw it away, and it just comes right back to you. Here are some stories of mamas who, with the spirit of generosity, felt inspired enough to throw a few boomerangs into the air.

## Adele's Story

My husband and I moved to Australia from Canada when our first two children were small, so that my husband could train as a chiropractor. My husband worked away a lot; as part of his training, he would travel to different clinics around Australia. He would often be gone for a few days at a time.

During one of his longer trips away (my second child was about five months old and my oldest was three years old), I ran into some trouble. I was bringing groceries in while holding Mia in my arms. I went to close the trunk, and, with both groceries and Mia in my arms, I did something to my back. I was in so much pain I couldn't lift up Mia to put her in her bed. I had a playpen, so I nursed her on the floor, then crawled to the playpen where I would tip the playpen over, roll her in the playpen, and stand it back up. My oldest couldn't even get his own drink, so I would have to push my body up to get him a drink. Whatever it was I had to do, it was just hideous. I was in the worst pain I've ever had in my whole life.

Later that day, my friend, Caroline, kept calling and calling. I didn't pick up the phone, so she called my husband's cell phone, and he said, "Can you go over and check on her—something must be wrong." She came over to find me crawling all over the house. She stayed with me until the kids were asleep. Though she was pregnant at the time, she put my kids to sleep and hung up my laundry that was sitting wet in the washing machine. Before she left, she made sure the kids were asleep in bed and gave me a glass of water. She was so nice; in fact, it was the nicest thing anyone had ever done for me. She saved the day because I literally could not pick up my baby and no one else was coming for me—not my husband, not my mom. I was on my own.

Caroline is like a bright light I will never forget. She knew I was in trouble, and she totally came to my rescue. Money could never buy the feeling of knowing that if I needed help, someone would show up for me.

When she went into labor and was having a really hard time, her mom called me to tell me she was in labor. I went right to the hospital and stayed with her. She was trying to stay calm and relaxed, and I tried to help her with some calming visualization exercises. Though her mom told me I didn't need to stay, I told her, "I'm staying until she sends me home."

—Adele

## Melissa's Story

I was so sad when my sister Rachel and her family recently moved away. It was really hard for me, because I felt like she was my safety blanket. Two years before, I had been so glad when my husband got accepted into school in the same city she was in. My husband was very busy with school and gone a lot of the time, leaving me at home with my two kids. My sister was kind of the person I would run to with all my worries and problems.

Because of that reliance, the news that she was moving was difficult. I had a really hard time being okay with it. But the thing that helped me the most was realizing that it was just as hard for her to have to move and leave everything behind. So I decided that instead of moping and feeling sorry for myself, I would go over and help her wherever I could, and it became almost an everyday thing. Sometimes I would be at her house all day so I could help her out with whatever she needed that day. That helped me focus on things other than myself, and it gave me comfort to know that it was something that had really blessed her. In the end, I felt a weight lifted because I had lifted hers.

One of the sweetest moments of service I've had the privilege of being a part of was while I was in Aberdeen after the birth of my second child. Having had such a difficult pregnancy, I felt it was my solemn duty to pay attention to the pregnant ladies I came in contact with. I listened, I validated, I told them they looked amazing, and acknowledged how horrible heartburn, backaches, desperate fatigue, water retention, and emotional instability were. Sitting in church about a month after Eliot was born, I turned to one such woman, Sarah, who was heavily pregnant with her first, and I asked how she was feeling. She burst into tears. We sat at the back of the room and whispered to each other throughout a good part of the lesson and then exchanged phone numbers.

She came and visited me in the mother's lounge the next Sunday and mentioned that she was nervous about having a baby and didn't know if she would know what to do with the baby once it came. She asked me about breastfeeding, and since I struggled with that as well, I was more than excited to tell her what I had learned. I thought that when the baby was born, I would be able to help her with that.

A few weeks later, she gave birth to a healthy baby boy. During the delivery, she suffered a stroke and a week after the delivery, she died. The Sunday after she passed, a woman handed me a bag filled with a few nursing-related items, among which was a pretty navy and white nursing bra. I had no idea where the items had come from as there were a number of young mothers in the community. When I thanked her and asked if she wanted any money for the things, she said, "Well, no, these things weren't able to be used for their intended purpose so . . ."

I realized that these were Sarah's, and it was tragic for me to think that Sarah didn't get a chance to nurse her little one. At first, I wasn't very keen on wearing the bra because I thought it would remind me of the tragedy, but I decided to wear it to remind myself of how lucky I was to be able to mother my children.

A few weeks later, I invited Sarah's husband over for dinner. He brought his little baby Logan with him, and I held and kissed and cuddled that little boy and wanted to cry thinking that his mother wasn't there to hold and kiss and cuddle him.

At one point in the evening, the baby started fussing and I knew he was hungry, so I asked if I could try feeding him. I took little Logan into my bedroom, unclasped Sarah's pretty navy and white bra, and nursed him. While I was attending to Logan, I had an overwhelming feeling that Sarah was there with us and that she was perhaps even orchestrating the help that needed to come to her husband and her baby. To connect like that to another mother who had passed away was an extraordinary experience.

## The More, the Merrier

You don't always have to go it alone when it comes to service. There is strength in numbers, and it's a great idea to look for groups who gather for the purpose of doing good.

An article in the *Corvallis Gazette Times*, entitled "Downing: Rural Women United as Happy Workers," describes how a group of rural women gathered, connected, and made a difference in one another's lives. Columnist Kathi Downing writes,

"Levis Pizer . . . recalls the hard life of the women in the 1920s and 30s [*sic*], living far from town without much money or a car or much contact with others. Most of their day was spent in gardening, preserving, sewing, cooking, caring for children. They were always hungry for news and the companionship of other women."[1]

Eleven women walked as far as a mile to attend a monthly gathering. The group grew the second month to nineteen, and then many more over the years. They called the group The Happy Workers Club. They enjoyed birthdays and baby showers. During the Second World War, they came together to sew items of clothing for soldiers and rolled bandages for the Red Cross. They became a force of action in their community, helping raise money for various causes—one of which was buying a schoolhouse. They also stepped up during community emergencies or crises.[2]

One member, Allison Pinkerton, wrote an article for the *Herald Tribune* entitled "Happily Making Quilts for Others." In the article, she writes about an Emmanuel Lutheran Church's Dorcas Quilting Mission. Over forty women meet together every Monday morning from October to April to sew quilts for Lutheran World Relief to distribute to those in need. They have what sounds like a well-oiled machine and are able to produce 750 quilts in one sewing season. The women divide into groups of sewers, cutters, and assemblers. They keep the patterns simple and focus on creating warmth for those who need it. The article states that "Lutheran World Relief quilts have been used for warmth, shelter and carrying children or possessions." Before the quilts go out they are dedicated with a prayer: "Bless this quilt and all who made it and all who will use it."[3]

The article interviewed sewers: Jackie Miller, Betty Keller, and Ann Dieter. "The women love the group and the fellowship it provides so much that Miller said they get anxious during the summer for meetings to resume. 'I love the companionship,' Betty Keller said as she worked at a sewing machine. As she cut fabric squares, Ann Dieter added, 'It's the highlight of my life.' Miller states, 'They enjoy what they're doing, they enjoy each other, and they're helping somebody else. What more could you ask for?'"[4]

These quilting ladies gathered to serve and were filled in return. They found purpose and camaraderie. There are opportunities wherever you are to serve like these ladies.

Last year, I received an e-mail from Karen, a member of the Cycling Mamas. She wrote to all of us in the group, hoping to organize supplies for a community center in Nicaragua. The e-mail read:

Hello Cycling Mamas!

I went on vacation to Nicaragua about a month or so ago. Besides being a great vacation destination, my family and I had the opportunity to share some time at a local soup kitchen and community centre near the area we stayed. The community centre is located in the village of Jiquilillo, but also services two other villages within walking distance. These villages are all about a forty-minute drive from the larger city of Chinandega (if you want to look on a map).

In speaking with the community centre staff, we asked what kinds of assistance they might want or need. They told us a number of options, and one that stood out for us, as a family, is sports equipment.

The Jiquilillo area has organized soccer and baseball leagues in which many, many children play. The structure of the league play is similar to what you would see here in Edmonton/Sherwood Park—BUT they play with no equipment! They play in bare feet and several teams share one soccer ball. The soccer and baseball "fields" are actually fields for animal grazing, and they chase the cows, pigs, and horses off when the teams play.

The people living in these villages are very poor, and cannot afford any equipment. So here it is . . . my family is gathering/collecting used soccer and baseball equipment to pack up and send over to this community centre we visited. If you have old shoes, shin pads, socks, gloves, baseballs, jerseys—really any equipment related to soccer or baseball—and you want to give it away to children and young adults in Nicaragua, please bring it to Cycling Mamas, and I will pack it up!

I want to thank you for even thinking about donating. I know there are so many incredible places and people who are in need—including here at home.

Take care, and see y'all at Cycling Mamas.

Karen

I was intrigued by Karen's e-mail and asked her how she got involved with volunteer projects in Nicaragua. She told me that she and her husband took their kids on a family vacation to Nicaragua and stayed at Monty's Beach Lodge. After visiting the website for Monty's Beach Lodge, I found out that this is a very special lodge. Guests that stay there have the opportunity to be connected with various service opportunities in the nearby villages. In 2006, the owner, Don Montgomery (a.k.a. Monty), backpacked around Nicaragua and fell in love with its natural beauty and the people who live there. He wanted to create a place where people from around the world could come, relax, and connect with the local people in meaningful ways.

In 2010, he established his palm-thatched lodge located in rural Nicaragua on a sandy North Pacific coastal surf beach. His ambitious vision has been realized. His guests can surf, kayak, explore mangroves, hike to volcanoes, and help meet local needs. Through the efforts of his guests working closely with local leaders, Monty has been able to build a health clinic, a community center, and classrooms for a local school. They are currently working on collecting school supplies, supporting local sports teams, building water filters, offering services from any visiting doctors or dentists, along with many other incredible endeavors.

Karen and her family have stayed at Monty's Beach Lodge several times. Speaking of her experiences there, she shared, "As a family, it was a gift for us to be able to share what we have with others."

Karen found that she and her family can satisfy a greater need within themselves when they serve others. Even on vacation—typically a time for personal rejuvenation—she has learned that reaching out to others brings happiness to her and her family. I have come to learn the same. The moments in my life when I am asking myself, "What can my village do for me?" are significantly less satisfying than the moments when I ask myself, "What can I do for my village?"

There are times as a mother when there doesn't seem like you have much excess to offer anyone. However, it might be possible, when you wonder what you can do for your village, to find little pockets of wealth that you can share with others.

Author Elizabeth Gilbert wrote a post about generosity on her Facebook page. She states, "Generosity is a state of being. It is a question of your spirit, not a question of your bank account. You're either a generous person, or you aren't. Some of the most generous people I've ever met were incredibly poor (at least financially—not in spirit). Some of the richest people I've ever met were not generous in the least—in fact, they clutch to their resources in constant terror of scarcity. . . . If you're waiting to become a billionaire before you become generous, I think you're missing the point."

There are so many ways to practice generosity. Whether your gesture is grand or meager, the act of being generous, in whatever form, will clean out the cobwebs of your heart and invigorate you in surprising ways. The spirit of generosity is definitely a friend of the village and can help you feel less lonely, because you can never touch another life without that life touching yours as well.

# ENDNOTES

1.  Kathi Downing, "Downing: Rural Women United as Happy Workers," *Corvallis Gazette-Times*, January 13, 2013, http://www.gazettetimes.com/news/local/downing-rural-women-united-as-happy-workers/article_80487962-5586-11e2-9f66-0019bb2963f4.html.

2.  Ibid.

3.  Allison Pinkerton, "Happily Making Quilts for Others." *Herald-Tribune*, February 6, 2012, http://www.heraldtribune.com/article/20120206/breaking/120209690.

4.  Ibid.

# CHAPTER 15

# Build Your Village During Business Hours

Whan I joined the Naval Reserves, I was sent to Saint-Jean-sur-Richelieu, Quebec, for Basic Military Training. One day, my platoon was doing physical training, and we were all lying on our backs in a circle doing sit-ups and leg lifts. We were all tired and spent, but our master corporal would not let us stop until everyone had done all the exercises.

At one point, we were asked to lift both our legs to a forty-five-degree angle. The exercise would not end until everyone managed to hold the position. I looked to my right, and the guy beside me was seriously struggling. Tired myself, I reached over to him with my own leg, put my leg under his, and lifted his leg up. I got yelled at for that, but the image has stuck with me, especially as a mother trying to reach out to others in need of help. Most days I can barely manage my own forty-five-degree angle—how on earth can I be expected to reach out and help anyone else?

There are times in life when you legitimately don't have many resources or much time to give, and inspiration is telling you to save your strength. Maybe you're grieving or physically incapacitated. Maybe you're in the middle of a nervous breakdown or just had your eighth child or are scrambling to make ends meet after the loss of a job. Giving other people your time and resources is a privilege not everyone can do at all times in their life. If there is even a tiny bit of space for it in your life, by all means, grab the opportunity. For those times when it seems that there's not, I think that working together, developing synergistic relationships, and weaving other women into your weekly or monthly rhythm is a great way to work village building into a busy life.

Most moms are busy. So when you are building or maintaining connections with others, it is wise to try to be productive while spending your valued time with your fellow villagers. I have found the best way to make and keep connections has been to weave other women into the very fabric of my life. If we both need to cook suppers, we cook together; if we both need to exercise, we exercise together; if we need to get groceries, we take turns looking after the kids while the other gets groceries. While there will be times when you will need to go out of your way to connect with others, I see two good reasons why combining village building with productivity is the ideal.

• Your village will change as people move in and out of your life.

• Being engaged in productive and meaningful work is an existential necessity.

## Dynamic Villages

When an old and beloved friend moves away, I do mourn the loss of the hours spent to build that relationship. I hate that I have no history with the woman who moves in. And I don't have lots of time to set aside to get to know new neighbors. But I do have time to meet her at the park so the kids can play. I do have time to talk with her as we cycle around the block.

We have to make our village building as efficient as possible because at any point in time, members of our constructed village could leave. It may be because of a job transfer or a house move or pass away. Life is unpredictable.

Our communities more closely resemble a river as opposed to a lake—people come and go and come and go. Admittedly, this isn't just a challenge unique to our day; it is the nature of life. Before cross-country job transfers, out of state universities, or international travel, there were wars and rampant diseases, and early deaths were not uncommon. In modern times, however, the river's flow seems to be dangerously fast paced, and rather than having a safety net of family and community to provide backup for those inevitabilities of life, we find ourselves having to start over from scratch again and again.

A friend of mine who is living in Los Angeles was lucky enough to have four other families with young kids living in their neighborhood. The families were good friends; they celebrated birthdays together, held potlucks, and swapped yard work duties. But this past summer, my friend was devastated to learn that three of the four families were moving away. She was then faced with the task of having to construct her village all over again. Her village is still under construction.

Our society is so transient that it can be exhausting putting so much work into building your village only to have it decimated again and again. However, when you can overlap your daily work with your networking, it is easier to find the time to reconstruct a village of support. And it expedites the process as well, strengthening friendships in the thick of life's happenings.

## Whistle While You Work

Meaningful work is an essential component of a happy life. Our sense of self and value are intimately entwined with a sense of purpose. When we multitask building our village and doing meaningful work, we strengthen our own sense of self as well as connect on a deeper, more intimate level with our sisters.

There is a big conversation today as mothers talk or write about trying to disconnect from many social media sites—which can compete with their children for their attention—and their words are usually laden with guilt. However, I believe that one reason the pull of social media is so strong is because many mothers are often desperate for not just amusement; they are desperate for connection, to remain relevant, and to be a valuable part of some type of work or social group. Connecting with our kids is vital, but so is fulfilling our needs for belonging and worthwhile work.

For the larger part of the great motherhood story of humankind, a mother's days have not been spent following their children around all day. Instead, the story has been that children followed their mothers around all day. Offspring joined their mothers in the fields while women grew essential food for their families, they sat at their mothers' feet while women spun cloth or molded clay into pottery.

A big struggle for me as a mother has been the realization that as a stay-at-home mom, the work I find myself unwillingly pushed toward the most is taking care of and cleaning all of the stuff that we own. Many of the times I've scolded my kids have been because they haven't properly taken care of my stuff or because they've damaged or lost their own.

"No jumping on the furniture."

"No running in the living room."

"No climbing on the rails."

"No touching the picture frames."

I've said these things to my children, all the while very aware that their job as kids is primarily to jump, run, climb, and touch as much stuff as they can. That's how they learn about their world. That's how they get stronger and smarter.

When I take my kids outside (which is always my preference), it is never lost on me that they become mesmerized by the act of throwing rocks into a nearby body of water. There is so much fun, learning, and growth in that activity—with no cleanup required. When they go for a walk in the river valley to find the biggest sticks they can or to climb some trees, there is no cleanup required. When we grab some food and eat our lunch at a park, I don't have to sweep or mop any floors.

Some women find cleaning and maintaining their home meaningful, perhaps because they are good at it, and it is a way of sharpening some skills they naturally have. That's great. Even important for them. Full steam ahead, then. But for me, the idea of spending a decade or more just cleaning and cleaning and cleaning is my own little tailored nightmare. The work rings hollow for me, because living that way is not really me focusing on my kids or honing a natural talent or ability—it's just me focusing on my stuff. I can't make a satisfying career out of that because, honestly, I just don't care about my stuff that much.

Things I do care about include teaching and loving my children, connecting with other mothers, reading, and writing. These passions have led how I shape my days. I am a stay-at-home mom who is writing a book about connecting with other moms based on my experiences. When I need to write, I often take my kids to some outside space with some books, paper, and pens. Instead of cleaning up after them, I let them do their work (the business of playing and exploring) while I do mine (the business of reading and writing). That path feels right to me.

Of course, there are many women who would find a morning of reading and writing unsatisfying and unproductive, and rightly so. It would ring hollow for them because that would not be investing in something that they care about. This is where I am coming from when I talk about meaningful work. Meaningful work will look different for each woman due to the diverse group of women that we are. We have the opportunity and joy to discover how we can incorporate meaningful work into our lives as mothers, and it is even more powerful when we can introduce productivity into our relationships with other moms.

Although I enjoy the introverted experience of writing, I also need to be part of a community. The moments in mothering when I have developed a coworker relationship with another mother and when I know that my presence in her life is important and impactful are fulfilling moments of worthwhile work for me. That is true even if that work is helping her clean her house, because then my work is not about my stuff; my work is about recognizing and caring about someone else's needs, as well as providing an opportunity for my children to connect with other children.

I sometimes see mothers in a difficult spot, having to regularly choose between basic needs: to be present and a part of their child's upbringing or being able to feel a part of a community while engaged in meaningful work. Though some say that a mom, alone at home all day, can always pick up the phone to ward off feelings of isolation and loneliness, that line of thought does not really acknowledge the undeniable feeling of disconnect many mothers experience. For many mothers, loneliness isn't about the need for idle chitchat. It is about the feeling of not being a productive and appreciated part of a group, team, or network.

Although I do understand our attraction to social media, I think online connections, although partially satisfying, are ultimately hollow connections when compared to actual face-to-face exchanges. However messy, real-life exchanges offer the human experience of love, patience, forgiveness, tolerance, kindness, and sacrifice. The happiness that comes from working with and for your fellow sisters is unmatched by any Facebook update, regardless of how many likes you get. Shared experiences are a deeper and more honest way of bonding with others. It is as my friend says:

> Becoming a mother has added a beauty to me that I don't think I would have found otherwise. It has taught me the joy that can be had in sharing a heavy load with another mother. The importance of this principle, I didn't fully understand until I was in the thick of my mothering experience.
>
> —Kate

As I have already mentioned, there is a lot of value in the mom-and-tots groups and toddler music or gymnastic classes out there (they are fantastic places to network). While there is a lot that they do offer, I see them as starting places rather than staying places, because they don't provide opportunities for challenging and fulfilling work for women. They don't offer the opportunity for the camaraderie offered in an environment of working together toward common goals. Many women have a hard time showing up with their toddler only to sit around and idly chat their mornings away (which can be very nice at times but is not, and never will be, a sufficient substitute for being engaged in meaningful work). A network of women pursuing purposeful work—whether that is as public as community service or as private as scrubbing each other's bathtubs—does not have to be large to be effective. Some women need only one or two close friends to feel emotionally and socially fulfilled. What matters is not the breadth of your network, but the depth that you're willing to go to for other women and their needs.

Our time and resources are limited. Our villages are dynamic and changing. But as we develop the habit of multitasking village building with our daily work, then it becomes easier to welcome new women into our lives and incorporate them into our lives in fulfilling ways.

Working side-by-side, even in less than ideal circumstances, can offer connection in a completely different way; connections with others over shared projects, tasks, and difficulties are deep and memorable. In doing this, we can build our villages while developing our talents, strengthening our skill sets and developing our sense of self. When the time is right, I highly recommend incorporating others into your life in productive and efficient ways.

# CHAPTER 16

# Weaving Your Life with the Lives of Other Women

Nicholas A. Christakis and James H. Fowler, authors of the book *Connected*, ask their readers to imagine that their house was on fire and that there is a lake a short distance away. All you have in your hands is a bucket. As you run from the lake to the house, back and forth, alone, spilling water from the bucket as you run, it is obvious that you will never be able to put the fire out. The authors then ask you to consider the task if there were a hundred people with you, running back and forth from the lake to the house—a much more effective setup for fighting the fire. The authors then offer one more scenario in which everyone organizes themselves and forms a bucket line from the burning house to the lake, continuously passing full buckets up the line and empty buckets back down. The authors illustrate how powerful working together in an organized way can be.

Right now it seems as though there are many mothers frantically running from the lake to their homes all by themselves, giving their all to the task at hand, yet ultimately feeling alone, overwhelmed, and angry the entire time.

A friend of mine once told me that when you are in the busy whirlwind of life with kids, you have to treat connecting with others as seriously as you would a doctor's appointment. She said marking dates (big cooks, date night parties, job shares) on your calendar and prioritizing them is a good start. I think her advice is wise.

When I began writing this book, I attempted to collectively mother for a week with three other moms as an experiment in cooperative mothering in our modern society. I wrote out an outline of what our days would look like intertwined for five days. Each of the days would be spent in a different woman's home, so we could provide housework for all women participating. There would be time scheduled for exercise, running errands, connecting with our kids, housework, and preparing an evening meal to take home.

All mothers who were invited to participate expressed interest and excitement about our proposed week together. It was, however, extremely tricky to find a week that worked for all of us. After multiple back-and-forth e-mails, we had decided on a week that wasn't perfect but was workable.

A few weeks before our experiment, I received an e-mail from one of the mothers: "I feel so bad backing out, but I don't think I can participate that week. We have had some plumbing and renovation needs come up, and I need to leave my week open to take care of those issues."

Another mother expressed that the scheduled week wasn't ideal, because her son had some important things happening that week that she had forgotten about and thought perhaps a different week would be better.

The third mother wrote, "I will be only a few days away from my due date, so I think I am out."

It was a nice idea. Looking back at this now, I see how flawed the idea is for most mothers. Our lives are so varied. Many work part- or full-time, and others might enjoy parts of it but not the entire experience (for instance, an extreme introvert might go nutso with all the "together time"). I also think it's weird that I thought we could schedule connecting with kids because connecting is often done in surprise moments or during teaching moments that come up in natural, unscheduled ways.

Like I said, it was a nice idea.

Despite the fact that I couldn't really make this work, the endeavor was not a fruitless one. When I came up with this idea, I was on the right track. I knew I wanted to weave other women into my life; I just wasn't sure how to make that happen. But just trying to organize that week helped me put down on paper what I needed help with as a mother: meals, appointments, opportunities for exercise, a break. I also learned that the best way to incorporate others into your life is by working with the flow of your life and weaving women in where it makes sense.

Setting up weekly commitments with specific women with whom I was interested in fostering a relationship has been a key component for my own village building. It is too easy for weeks to fly by without touching base with those you care about. But that doesn't happen if they are scheduled into your week with a regular activity that equally fills a need for you and her.

In addition to revolving weekly or monthly get-togethers, I found it worked well to invite other families into our lives with things like carpooling or playing soccer in the park.

Last year, with everything I had learned about the importance of creating community in my life, I stockpiled community as if I were heading toward a zombie apocalypse. I held book clubs, date night parties, music evenings, big cooks, kid swaps, and joined my beloved Cycling Mamas group. That sounds like a lot of work, but last year was a busy year for us as well—my husband and I didn't have fountains of extra time on our hands—so I multitasked as much as possible. I wanted to avoid the unsatisfying kind of busyness that our family can get swept away in, which meant taking time to identify the needs of every member of the family and then making intentional choices about what I said yes to and what I said no to.

For the rest of this chapter, I offer examples of combining productivity with village building in the hopes that they will help you come up with ideas that would best suit your own families.

## Couples' Book Club

Forget dinner parties that require a lot of cooking and cleaning; I have enough of that in my life already. I decided that I wanted people in my home, not to eat my food, but to fill my living room with lively discussions about poetry, short stories, or essays. (No one in our club has time for a novel a month—or even a novel every six months.)

This came together organically one day when we were visiting with some old friends at a barbecue. These were people who lived in our city but not close to our neighborhood. The couples in our group offered to take turns hosting, so it wasn't always us tidying up the house every time. We still try to meet once a month. Some months slip past us, but it is a great way to include these friends into the rhythm of our lives. Since it is a couples' book club, it's also a night out for Jordan and me. The kids usually come with us, and we put a movie on somewhere while we chat with other adults.

This has been a very inexpensive way to connect with others. I get a date night with my spouse, friend time, and great conversation about literature, all in one evening.

## Music Night

We have also held music nights a few times. I play the piano, and I love to sing. My husband plays the guitar and the double bass. This is a common interest for us, something we can both look forward to and participate in with equal enthusiasm, which means this is also good for our marriage. My sons are also taking piano lessons, and I want them to see that their hard work can be joyful and fun when they are able to play their instruments with other people.

These evenings further a few family goals for us: building community, developing talent, having family fun, and growing common interests as a couple. On my music nights, I invited *anyone* I knew who played an instrument or sang to my small home, copied some music for different instruments, and we just went through the music together.

One Christmas season, I had in my living room a cheerful gathering of people playing various instruments and singing. The instruments included a violin, a cello, three guitars, a trumpet, and a piano. I also managed to include a woman who sang in local theater productions. This wasn't a group of common friends—I scrounged this group together from book club friends, church, and family. We all had a love of music in common and that was enough, I think. On that especially memorable dark, snowy winter night, my living room was transformed into a warm, beautiful melodic haven, filled with

"O Holy Night," "Fairytale of New York," an attempt at Handel's *Messiah*, and more. Music night is beautiful and satisfying for our whole family.

# Date Night Party

I got the idea of date night parties from my sister, who started hosting them on a monthly basis. A date night party is an evening where I offer to watch neighborhood kids so that their parents can go on a date. This one was a little tricky for me, and while my amazing sister made homemade pizza for her guests, I streamlined the work involved and offered chips and hotdogs. I found that warmer days were the best times for us to host these, as I could keep all the kids in my backyard. (I try to avoid situations with large amounts of cleanup as much as possible.)

It has been a mutually beneficial thing for our neighbors and our family as our kids *love* date night parties. Date night parties meet some of their important social needs, too.

The idea is simple: find some couples with young families who seem like they would appreciate a night out without having to hire a babysitter (which can get quite costly). They drop their kids off in your backyard for a few hours and take off. I set up several activities for the kids: a trampoline, sidewalk chalk, a LEGO table, and some soccer balls and nets. My husband especially enjoys any child who shows even a tiny interest in kicking a ball into a net, and so he generally oversees soccer drills with the kids.

This idea is a little more work and isn't always as pleasurable for the hosting adults, but if you are looking for an opportunity for service in your life and are finding it hard to do with a bunch of kids, this is one that is very doable. You are giving your friends space to strengthen their marriages and village building as well.

The times we've done this definitely helped us to connect with other young families, and, while we were not looking for any kind of payback, we appreciated when others invited our kids over for a date night party, so my husband and I could also go out.

# Connecting and Cooking

There are women who gather for big cooks with friends and prepare meals for a month. Big cooks are a great idea but can be intimidating. In fact, a friend of mine posted on Facebook that they wanted to do a big cook, and I jumped at the idea . . . so did a few others. We tried to organize a date, the menu to cook, who was going to get the groceries, and sort out food allergies. It was a lot of work, and then it eventually fell apart because . . . who knows? A million reasons. Busy moms trying to coordinate large projects with each other is a really hard thing to do; it's not impossible, but it can get pretty tricky. Big cooks might work for others, and I would like to give it a go someday, but so far, with my time constraints, big group cooks just do not work for me.

What does work looks a little different than what I'd originally envisioned. One day, I was over visiting my back-alley buddy. Our kids were playing together, and my friend asked if I wanted to make soup with her. She is a fly-by-the-seat-of-her-pants kind of girl, so we work well together. I ran down the back alley and grabbed anything at home that I had to make soup, and she went through her fridge and did the same. We ended up making hamburger soup with various vegetables. It was a hit. I got a great visit in with a cherished friend of mine, provided a social opportunity for my children while they played with her children, and was able to multitask that with making our family's evening meal.

We have done this more than once, and most times, it was an impromptu thing. I don't know if it would have worked any other way for me.

# When You're Working Outside the Home

Having evenings and weekends as the only time available to village build can present challenges. My friend Virginia shared that one challenge of working full-time was that she was so tired after working all day it was hard for her to pull out the energy required to work on friendships.

Just as the Inuit dialect in northern Canada have several words for snow, I think mothers need more than one word for tired. Just a few examples:

1.  I-got-woken-up-twice-last-night tired.

2.  I-was-up-*all*-night tired.

3.  I-deal-with-being-tired-by-subsisting-on-chocolate-and-haven't-exercised-in-months tired.

4.  I-listened-to-a-toddler-whining-all-day tired.

5.  I-listened-to-my-*twin*-toddlers-whining-all-day tired.

6.  I'm-busy-all-day-at-work-and-then-come-home-and-have-a-second-shift-with-the-kids-and-the-house-and-then-grocery-shopping-at-9:00-at-night tired.

7.  My-teenager-fights-me-on-everything tired.

8.  I-feel-stretched-too-thin-and-our-financial-worries-are-crushing-me tired.

There are a lot of tired mamas out there. Because Virginia was feeling so tired and because her time was so limited, she found it essential to connect while being productive.

She mentioned that she was able to find good village members through her kids. Sending her kids to a community school has helped with that. Some schools offer parents a list of names and contact information for other parents in your child's class—if you get one of those, put that gem in a safe place. If your school doesn't do that, then organize one, like a mom did for Will's kindergarten class. When you take your kids to the park, you could use the list to throw out an invite to parents to join you for a little soccer game there. You could also fairly easily pick up some fast food and invite other parents to do the same for a picnic at a playground after work. The kids eat and play while you make connections. There's no food to cook, dishes to clean up, counters to wipe, or floors to sweep.

My friend also found that going to community league events helped her to get to know the people in her neighborhood better. Here in Edmonton, each neighborhood has a community league building. The leagues host craft sessions, Halloween parties, yoga, plant swaps, game nights, and more. The events vary, depending on the interests of the neighborhood. Volunteering with this group also means an opportunity to connect. Sometimes it pays off to drop by a community event, even if it is outside of your interests, for the opportunity to meet some community faces. Some community leagues offer opportunities for people to get involved with community gardens, which families can work on together on the weekends.

Our community league has an ice rink. During the winter months, they need volunteers to watch over the rink when it's in use. My husband signed up for one shift a week as he thought it would be a good way to help out our community and schedule in some outdoor exercise for our family. It turned out well. We have met other volunteers in our community from this experience and have been able to meet up with friends from school whom we've invited to join us during our shift.

A little shack sits three steps from the rink for volunteers to warm up, drink hot chocolate, and relax—there's even a TV and a cozy couch in there. It was a highlight of the week for our boys to be able to man the shack. Though it was sometimes a fight to get everyone dressed and out the door, when we got there, peace and happiness reigned. I'm not overstating that peace and happiness bit; I even wrote to my friends on Facebook after an especially beautiful evening skate: "Tonight as I unlaced my skates and put my boots back on, I was distracted by the hanging Christmas lights that are strung up across the Fulton Place community outdoor ice rink. Magical. And as I was walking home, I turned back to gaze at the scene, and from the speakers, I heard, 'It's the most wonderful time of the year.'" That community volunteer opportunity turned out to be a wise investment of our time.

Local after-school activities can also be a good place to connect with other parents and even set up carpools—a big time-saver for busy moms. When it's your turn to do the driving, you may find that showing up to matches or games can lead to village building. My cousin, who is a nurse and mother of four active kids, was recently telling me how much she and her husband (a pilot) enjoyed driving her kids to their basketball games. Their lives seemed complicated with unconventional work schedules and four kids. I asked her how she finds the time to build her village. Her answer was simple: the other parents at the basketball games were a big part of their family village. They would cheer together and celebrate together. Playing a sport helped the kids bond with their teammates' parents as well, offering them much needed adult backups in their lives.

My friend Virginia also offered this:

> Sometimes when time is tight, you have to take what you can get. One of the reasons I have been able to keep a strong friendship with one of my closest mom friends is that she is willing to have a strong relationship with me through texting. Sometimes we have these huge text conversations; it's not as good as face-to-face, but it's that or nothing. I really feel like I've developed a bond with her, and we have these great conversations where I feel like I get real comfort from her. If one of us has a problem, we work through it together; but because we don't have an hour to put into it, we put in that hour over two days via text until the problem is solved.

Whether time is plentiful or short, the initial work of weaving others into your life will take some effort and creativity, but as soon as you are able to develop some good friendships, it will stop being work, as those friendships will be strong supports for you and your family.

# CHAPTER 17

# A World of Moms Yearning for a Village

After school today, my children told me that a local playwright and actress came to their school and talked about her work. The kids then told me that she had written, directed, and acted in an entire play all by herself. Astonishingly, she somehow played every character that was in her production. I've never seen this particular play—it's probably very clever and amazing—but in the rushed moment I was in listening to my kids explain her performance, I couldn't help wondering why she didn't just grab some extra actors and actresses to help her out. Aren't there a plethora of actors and actresses hungry for parts and willing to perform for free . . . everywhere?

The idea of trying to play every part may seem absurd, but there are many moms who attempt this same feat. As I've collected stories of mothers who have shown up for each other and make guest appearances as allomothers, I see how much richer of an experience this is for both the cast and the audience members. All of our mothering experiences could be less stressful with more than just one actress on stage trying her best to play every part.

Here's a story from a mother of five children—two of which have been diagnosed with psychological disorders—who recognized her need to weave her life together with other women.

> Guilt. We all feel it as parents. When I feel guilt it's often because I'm comparing myself to others—competing with them, rather than focusing on building a community.

This lesson hit home for me last November. One of my children had come home from school for lunch and announced she wasn't going back to school. This is my child with a mood disorder, so her demands weren't unusual. She hates school. However, I did find it a bit unusual because it was her birthday. So many great things happen to you at school on your birthday. In response to her declaration, I spurted my string of usual responses: "Of course you are. I know you don't like school, but in our family we go to school. You can have a break later in the week, but you must go today."

Her behaviors escalated, and pretty soon she was yelling at me and slamming the doors. I didn't have my van that day (it was in the shop for an oil change), so I told her I was getting the stroller out and putting her little siblings in the stroller, and she needed to be ready to go by the time I was ready. You must understand, I live in Canada, and this was a cold day and it was no small feat to walk to her school, but I was determined. I got back into the house (half frozen) only to find this child in the bathroom with the door locked.

*Deep breath.* No problem, I will just pop the safety. No go. She was holding the lock from the inside. She wasn't going anywhere. I was pretty much fuming at this point. I brought the little ones back in and called her dad to vent. There was really only one thing left to do. I had to wait her out. I started having fun with the little kids, hoping that would draw her out. An hour-and-a-half later, she came out. There was about an hour left of the afternoon, and so I told her she had two choices: go to school and have a fun break later or sit in the bathroom till after school time. She chose to stay in the bathroom, complaining (very loudly) about what a terrible mother I was and how this was the worst day ever.

The guilt hit. I was a terrible mother. It was her birthday, and I was forcing her to spend the rest of the afternoon in the bathroom. I really didn't know how to mother her. I wanted to celebrate her and the special day and her role in our family, but I knew letting her out was inviting a repeat incident. I had to stick to my guns on this one, and I knew it.

Just before three o'clock, someone came to the door. It was her teacher from church. She had come to drop off a birthday gift for her. I invited the woman in, telling her that my daughter was actually home even though school wasn't done yet. They had a brief but delightful interaction, and my daughter was the proud new owner of a dart gun and a bubble gum dispenser. The teacher left, and my girl was on top of the world.

I called the woman later, thanking her profusely. You see, in that moment she had done what I couldn't. I had to hold my ground and enforce a consequence for a bad choice which, in the long run, was good for her. But in the short term, I needed someone to boost her self-esteem and make her feel important on her big day. I needed another mother. Luckily, I had another member of my community who was there when we needed her, and I will be forever grateful for the mothers who bear with me on this journey.

There are times, like this story illustrates, when you do need someone else to step in and be a part of your children's lives. Many are lucky enough to have family close enough to connect with in that way. Here's a story from a woman who made deliberate choices to encourage her family to live close to her. For them, a more communal way of mothering has turned out to be a very successful arrangement.

My husband and I first bought our house in the Ottwell area, and we really loved the neighborhood, so whenever one of our brothers or sisters were looking for a house to buy in our city, we found houses for them to look at, usually no farther than a couple blocks from us. Now, I have two sisters and a sister-in-law living just a few blocks from each other.

Through the years, depending on needs, we took turns helping each other. My sister-in-law, Cindy, and I actually first lived together in a house with our families; we rented the basement, and they were upstairs. Our first babies were just three weeks apart. We left our doors open, and the kids would go up and down between the two floors all day long. We loved that if one of our kids were napping, I could just leave the baby monitor with Cindy and go shopping or vice versa.

When we bought our first house and moved out of that basement, we both missed having that second mom in the house, so they bought a house just a couple blocks away. When our first two children were going to kindergarten, she would drop them off for me because I just had a new baby. That was such a blessing. We also swapped kids one day a week. Monday was her day to get things done, and Wednesday was mine. One day a week would be a kids-free day.

For years, Mandi (my other sister who only lives a few blocks away) and I would swap Friday nights. One Friday night she and her husband would drop off their kids and have a night out, and the next Friday night we would drop our kids off at their house and go on a date. It was free babysitting, plus the cousins got to be good friends. Now the kids are all great friends and can go between houses and walk to school together.

We've also done lunch swaps—taking turns picking up kids from the school, feeding them lunch, and dropping them off. That meant that two days a week you'd have five kids for lunch, but for two days you wouldn't have any.

It's kind of like a pay-it-forward thing, too. Sometimes things didn't feel even when Cindy took all three of my kids, and I only took her one; I felt guilty because I thought, "This isn't fair for you, right?" Little did we know that, years later, I now watch her kids, and she feels it isn't fair because I have no kids for her to watch. Sometimes I watch her kids, and she says, "Can you babysit them today? I have errands, but I hate that I can never return the favor for you," and I'm thinking, "Don't you remember when you used to take all mine?"

Pitching in to mother or mentor other children and paying service forward can be extremely rewarding. In addition to being rewarding, working cooperatively is smart.

> Research demonstrates that cooperation surely brings out the *best* in us. This finding has been held in virtually every occupation, skill, or behavior tested. For instance, scientists who consider themselves cooperative tend to have more published articles than their competitive colleagues. Cooperative businesspeople have higher salaries. From elementary grades to college, cooperative students have higher grade point averages. Personnel directors who work together have fewer job vacancies to fill. And, not surprisingly, cooperation increases creativity. Unfortunately, most people are not taught cooperative skills.[1]

If you find yourself in a spot where you need both help and friendship, I think a good first step is to consider what resources you have to offer other people. When intentionally creating working relationships with others, try to find solutions that benefit both parties equally to ensure the sustainability of your working relationships. Of course, there will be times when you give more to others (which can be good for the soul) and perhaps times when others seem to be able to give more to you, but as much as possible, try to configure mutually beneficial arrangements.

At Christmastime, I was able to listen to my two sisters-in-law, Melissa and Lindsay, work out such an arrangement for themselves. They both live in the same city, but are not neighbors. Melissa works part-time and has four school-aged children. Lindsay is a full-time stay-at-home mom and has a one-year-old. Their lives as mothers look very different, so they were finding it difficult to find the time to connect with each other.

As they took the time to talk over the situation, they were able to communicate things they needed, as well as things they could offer each other. Lindsay had studied music in her undergraduate degree and then got a teaching degree. Since she was missing teaching music, as well as her nephews and her sister, Lindsay decided that she would really enjoy going over to Melissa's home once a week and helping her nephews practice their instruments. While she did this, the nephews not in a practice session would be able to entertain and look after her little one-year-old, leaving Melissa to be able to have some extra time to make supper. This arrangement gave Lindsay a break from chasing after her one-year-old and allowed her the time for needed connection with her family on a regular basis. This was a win for her, a win for her sister, and a win for the kids.

While service is an important part of everyone's life, mutually beneficial solutions to problems can be more sustainable for longer periods of time; they are the smartest way for you to source help for yourself. Think of things you can offer someone else before you ask for help. Maybe you are a whiz in the kitchen and can offer to make some meals (splitting the cost) in exchange for some babysitting. Or perhaps you are someone who can organize in a windstorm or teach lessons. Or maybe you have the time to make an online photo book for someone who doesn't have the patience for computers but is happy to work in your garden in exchange. If you make sure your exchange is truly beneficial for the other person as well as yourself, the arrangement will be more reliable and, as I've said before, longer lasting.

I enjoyed hearing from Angela, who started a mutually beneficial preschool group with some other moms.

> Joy School is a preschool program developed by Linda and Richard Eyre. The focus is on the joys of childhood: the joy of spontaneity and delight, the joy of curiosity, the joy of goal setting, etc. It just seemed like a natural curriculum for a lot of kids to be involved in. I organized a group of mothers, and we taught each other's children in our home twice a week and would rotate who taught and hosted. That was a fun way to connect with moms and kids. It was also a great way to help our kids feel welcome in other neighborhood homes.

Another friend of mine shared that, when she was young, her mother had a group of friends who took turns helping each other. Once a week, they would go over to someone's house and do a big job for them. One day the ladies would go, kids in tow, to one of their homes and wash all the walls in the house. The next week, they would go over to someone else's home and pick all the apples from their apple tree. While the women worked, the kids just came together and played. I loved this idea and appreciated that the women were more than friends; they were also colleagues.

With this aspiration in mind, my mornings were deliberately scheduled so that four days a week, I was committed to some sort of outside contact. Tuesdays and Thursdays, I had Cycling Mamas. Mondays and Fridays, I had organized weekly swaps with my friends Karen and Talia. I have already raved about the incredible benefit of Cycling Mamas, so I would like to take some time here to rave about *the swap*.

I almost want to write about swapping in the most reverent way possible— it meant that much to me. We organized it like this: my friend would drop her kids off for a few hours in the morning, pick them up before lunch, we would feed our kids separately, and then I would drop my kids off for a few hours in the afternoon. I loved this setup, because those other moms essentially became my coworkers. I saw them four times during the day, and it really felt like we were tackling our day together.

I also agreed to watch (for pay) my friend Bree's little girl on Monday mornings and all day on Wednesdays. Initially, I was hesitant to take on the job, because I thought it might be a bit much for me, but inviting her and her daughter into my weekly rhythm was the right choice. I considered our agreement to also be a swap of sorts; I just swapped for money rather than child care, which was also productive for my family.

Because we wove our workdays together in that way, we also wove in opportunities to have someone around to vent frustrations to or to talk out problems with or just to share a laugh with. We did all this while being productive.

The swaps I set up did not happen every single week, even though that is what we planned for. Kids get sick, moms get sick, and things come up. So, although it may seem like a lot to plan a swap every week, for me, it turned out to be less. In fact, an interesting thing happened one year with my swap coworkers.

The first half of the year ran like clockwork. I had my swaps, I had Cycling Mamas, and I was feeling like I was coming out of my funk, slowly but surely.

Then one day, one of my swap buddies suggested a hard-core military work out. I, of course, said, "Sounds good."

She was extremely cautious with me, and, despite her wise warnings to be careful to not push myself in ways that felt uncomfortable, I pushed myself in ways that felt uncomfortable. The next day, I could barely move my neck. I was in excruciating pain. It was a big deal. The pain was a pinched nerve in my neck, which radiated all the way down my right arm. It took a massive amount of effort even to click my computer mouse. I was down for the count.

My mom (saving me once again) came to my house and helped me through a very difficult first week. She helped when she could even after that. Despite going to chiropractors, doctors, physiotherapists, massage therapists, acupuncturists, and osteopaths, this injury took its sweet time to heal. I was in chronic pain for over four months. I couldn't help but feel a little angry, like I had been kicked in the teeth just as I was slowly starting to rise from my last blow.

You would think that that would be the end of my swaps, but miraculously, one of my swap buddies, Talia, had the time and energy to offer some service. She took my kids on our swap day without dropping hers off with me in the afternoon. I felt grateful and humbled and connected. I had made a friend I could count on during tough times, and my love for her grew.

Then, just as I was coming out of the worst of my injury and began feeling like I could function like a normal person, my friend Talia hurt her knee while hiking in Hawaii. She came back with crutches, so for the next little while I took her little one on our swap day without dropping any kids off at her house.

Then, bad luck descended on Karen. She had previously been diagnosed with a chronic illness, which was being kept at bay with medication. Suddenly, her disease progressed rapidly, putting her in the hospital with some bleak times ahead. Karen needed help, and, of course, Talia and I both jumped at the chance to help her and her husband with child care at a time when they desperately needed backup.

Around the same time, my friend Bree was growing larger and larger with every passing week—twins. She was overjoyed with her pregnancy but was surprised at how taxing the pregnancy was getting. She was a busy lady with two kids and a couple of part-time jobs, and she was exhausted. Taking care of her little one turned out great for me, because I had a playmate for my kids, I had some extra money, and I had an extra coworker stitched into my week. I also had the opportunity to provide consistent care for her little one, which offered her some peace of mind.

When things were looking tough for Bree, I offered to make a big batch of supper on Wednesdays to split between her family and mine. She paid for her portion of the food, didn't have to worry about supper at least one night a week, and we often had the opportunity to have a satisfying chat as she sat on my bar stool while I finished making supper.

Each of these swaps worked so easily because these ladies were already woven into my life.

The world is rich with need, and it can be surprising when you reach out to find how many needs you are able to meet while having your own met as well. This give-and-take is what was happening in the story of that happy table in the afterlife, with everyone's hands tied together as they all worked to feed one another. In reaching out to the other mamas in our great big world, you will have that same sweet opportunity to pick up your chopsticks and find heaven.

# ENDNOTES

1.   Perry Buffington, "Competition vs. Cooperation." Charles Warner. http://
     www.charleswarner.us/articles/competit.htm.

CHAPTER 18

# For the Islanders

There was a time in the history of this earth when all the continents and islands were one giant landmass. And then they drifted apart. As I've looked at mothers throughout the ages, it seems as though we have largely followed suit. However, we can't accept being stuck alone on our proverbial islands, because the truth is that *all* mothers will need backup at some point in their lives.

I recently was in touch with Sara, who is an extremely self-sufficient, capable, efficient woman. She is the kind of woman who can typically leap tall buildings with a single bound . . . while breastfeeding. Her three children are all under the age of seven—her youngest is eighteen months old—and she is seven months pregnant.

Recently, her superhuman bounds were barely getting her over the side of a bathtub. Her three-year-old daughter was extra needy (a pattern which had been developing over the previous few months) and was loudly whining as they were on their way out the door. An older neighbor stopped to say hello. She and Sara were chatting a bit, and Sara expressed how needy her three-year-old was being. The neighbor suggested that my friend just give her the extra attention she needed. The neighbor advised, "Just give it to her. She will probably start being easier if you just do that, because children need a lot of attention." As Sara finished relating this experience to me, she had only one question: "What if you don't have any more to give?"

As mothers, I think we are always searching for answers: how to get our babies to sleep through the night; how to get our four-year-old boys to stop peeing on the wall when they think it is hilarious; how to answer those impossible questions, like "Mom, what happens if a mosquito gets a needle and then also the earthquake?" Answers are sometimes hard to come by, but I think what is even more difficult to reconcile is knowing the answer, seeing what would help your child, and simply not being able to provide it.

The truth is that there will be times in every mother's journey when she feels she is simply not enough. I have also felt that I, alone, am not enough. However, this feeling doesn't make me feel guilty anymore, because I now know that *together, we are enough*.

That is what I want to share with my fellow islanders—all of you who may at times look out and see an ocean of nothingness. Together, we are enough.

I am a mother with three children—ages six, three, and ten months—with limited energy and time. I write during in-between moments while my baby grabs at my mouse and my three-year-old tells me he's done coloring and actually has three hundred questions that must be answered *now*. Maybe just before I start supper, I'll have a moment, or perhaps after the kids are in bed, I'll take some time. This is a piecemeal work done amid a hundred distractions. But while I am cleaning toilets, I think about these things. And while I lie down with my children before they drift off to sleep, I think about these things. And my thoughts in those scattered moments demand to be documented somewhere, because my heart heard them and was moved.

So this is my humble offering to the other mothers out there, a little note stuffed into a bottle and thrown out into an ocean of books on motherhood. My hope, however, is that maybe there is one lonely islander who picks it up after it washes to shore and feels in her heart that she is not alone.

# Acknowledgments

I'd like to express gratitude for my husband who, on many Saturdays, took all the kids to the park so I could write. I'm also very grateful to my mom, dad, mother-in-law, and friends who offered to look after my kids when big deadlines loomed.

I'm very grateful to all the women who shared their stories with me, those who offered to be beta readers, and those exceptionally patient ones who let me talk their ears off during the brainstorming stage of this book.

I also want to express my gratitude to two very patient, yet tenacious, editors who were able to see beauty in the mess I handed them.

Finally, I would also like to thank all the moms, grandmothers, aunts, and sisters who are a part of my own village. I love you all.

# Bibliography

Armstrong, Thomas. *Neurodiversity: Discovering the Extraordinary Gifts of Autism, ADHD, Dyslexia, and Other Brain Differences*. Cambridge, MA: Da Capo Press, 2010.

Alexander, Bruce K. "Addiction: The View from Rat Park (2010)." http://www.brucekalexander.com/articles-speeches/rat-park/148-addiction-the-view-from-rat-park.

Beck, Martha. "Yes? No? Maybe? How to Make Decisions." *Creating Your Right Life* (blog). September 29, 2013. http://marthabeck.com/2013/09/how-to-make-decisions/.

Berkowitz, Gale. "UCLA Study on Friendship Among Women: An Alternative to Fight or Flight." Anapsid.org. Last modified January 1, 2014. http://www.anapsid.org/cnd/gender/tendfend.html.

Bethune, Brian, and Genna Buck. "The Science Is In: God Is the Answer." *MacClean's*. March 2015. http://www.macleans.ca/society/science/god-is-the-answer/.

Betzig, Laura L., Alisa Harrigan, and Paul Turke. "Childcare on Ifaluk." *Zeitschrift für Ethnologie* 114 (1989): 161–177. http://www.jstor.org/stable/25842108.

Brazelton, T. Berry. *Learning to Listen: A Life Caring for Children*. Boston: Da Capo Press, 2013.

Buffington, Perry W. "Competition vs. Cooperation." Charles Warner. http://www.charleswarner.us/articles/competit.htm.

Butler, Samuel. "Joining and Disjoining." *Literature in English*. Edited by W. H. New and W. E. Messenger. Scarborough, Ontario: Prentice Hall Canada, 1993: 1088–1089.

Condradt, Larissa, and Timothy J. Roper. "Consensus Decision Making in Animals." *Trends in Ecology and Evolution* 20, no. 8 (August 2005): 449–456.

Cordes, Jill. "The Mom Mystique." *Parents*. August 16, 2013. http://www.parents.com/blogs/fearless-feisty-mama/2013/08/16/must-read/the-mom-mystique/ (site discontinued).

Covey, Stephen. *The 7 Habits of Highly Effective People: Powerful Lessons in Personal Change*. New York: Simon & Schuster, 1989.

Crittenden, Ann. *The Price of Motherhood*. New York: Metropolitan Books, 2001.

Downing, Kathi. "Downing: Rural Women United as Happy Workers." *Corvallis Gazette-Times*. January 3, 2013. http://www.gazettetimes.com/news/local/downing-rural-women-united-as-happy-workers/article_80487962-5586-11e2-9f66-0019bb2963f4.html.

Drexler, Peggy. "Why There Are More Walk-Away Moms." CNN. May 6, 2013. http://www.cnn.com/2013/05/04/opinion/drexler-mothers-leaving/.

Flinthart, Aiki. *The Yu Dragon*. Amazon Digital Services, Inc., 2012.

"Fractalism." Facebook. n.d. https://www.facebook.com/fractalstateofmind.

Forlanski, Tamara, and Lara Schroeder. "Lisa Gibson Drowned Her Children and Took Her Own Life: Police." *Global News*. October 4, 2013. http://globalnews.ca/news/880180/police-classify-case-of-gibson-mom-kids-a-homicide/.

Green, Linda. *Fear as a Way of Life: Mayan Widows in Rural Guatemala*. New York: Columbia University Press, 1999.

Granger, Liz. "Cancer—When Good Cells Go Bad." *The Brain Bank* (blog). March 11, 2013. http://thebrainbank.scienceblog.com/2013/03/11/cancer-when-good-cells-go-bad/.

Hanauer, Cathi. *The Bitch in the House: 26 Women Tell the Truth About Sex, Solitude, Work, Motherhood, and Marriage*. New York: Harper Collins Publishers, 2013.

Harees, Lukman. *The Mirage of Dignity on the Highway of Human 'Progress': The Bystanders' Perspective*. Bloomington, Indiana: AuthorHouse.

"How Do Cells Work Together in the Human Body?" *McGraw Hill Resources: Topic 1.3*. Whitby, Ontario: McGraw Hill Education, 2014.

Hrdy, Sarah. *Mothers and Others: The Evolutionary Origins of Mutual Understanding*. Cambridge: Harvard University Press, 2011.

Kendall-Tackett, Kathleen. *How Other Cultures Prevent Postpartum Depression: Social Structures that Protect New Mothers' Mental Health*. Uppity Science Chick. http://www.uppitysciencechick.com/how_other_cultures.pdf.

King, Martin Luther Jr. "Remaining Awake through a Great Revolution." Speech given at Oberlin College, Oberlin, OH. June 1965. http://www.oberlin.edu/external/EOG/BlackHistoryMonth/MLK/CommAddress.html.

Kermoian, Rosanne, and P. Herbert Leiderman. "Infant Attachment to Mother and Child Caretaker in an East African Community." *International Journal of Behavioral Development* 9 (1986): 455–469.

Luthar, Suniya S. "The Culture of Affluence: Psychological Costs of Material Wealth." *Child Development* 74, no. 6 (2003): 1581–1593.

Myers, David G.. *The American Paradox: Spiritual Hunger in an Age of Plenty.* New Haven, CT: Yale University Press, 2000.

Martin, JoAnn. "Motherhood and Power: The Production of a Women's Culture of Politics in a Mexican Community." *American Ethnologist* 17, no. 3 (August 1990): 470–490. doi: 10.1525/ae.1990.17.3.02a00040.

Moores, D. J. "Mystical Discourse in Wordsworth and Whitman: A Transatlantic Bridge." Leuven, Belgium: Peeters Publishers, 2006.

Napikoski, Linda. "Collective Mothering: Does It Take a Mother to Raise a Child?" AboutEducation. http://womenshistory.about.com/od/ feministtexts/a/collective_mothering.htm.

O'Brien, Barbara. "Prince Siddhartha: The Prince Who Became the Buddha." AboutReligion http://buddhism.about.com/od/Gautama-Buddha/fl/ Prince-Siddhartha.htm.

Robertson, Emma, Nalan Celasun, and Donna E. Stewart. "Risk Factors for Postpartum Depression. In Donna E. Stewart, E. Robertson, Cindy-Lee Dennis, Sherry L. Grace, and Tamara Wallington. *Postpartum Depression: Literature Review of Risk Factors and Interventions.* Toronto: University Health Network Women's Health Program, 2003.

Pinkerton, Allison. "Happily Making Quilts for Others." *Herald-Tribune.* February 6, 2012. http://www.heraldtribune.com/article/20120206/ breaking/120209690.

Roosevelt, Theodore. "Address to the New York State Agricultural Association." Speech given in Syracuse, NY. September 7, 1903. http://www.presidency. ucsb.edu/ws/?pid=24504.

Steinbeck, John. *East of Eden.*

"The Complete Works of Swami Vivekananda." WikiSource. n.d. https:// en.wikisource.org/wiki/The_Complete_Works_of_Swami_Vivekananda/ Volume_3/Lectures_from_Colombo_to_Almora/The_Work_before_us.

The Milpa Project. http://www.themilpaproject.com/the_team.html.

Thurston, Karyn. "Ten True Things about the First Year of Parenthood." *Girl of Cardigan* (blog). November 5, 2013. http://www.girlofcardigan.com/ten-true-things-about-the-first-year-of-parenthood/.

Todd, Charlie. "The Shared Experience of Absurdity." Filmed May 2011. TED Talk, 12:04. https://www.ted.com/talks/charlie_todd_the_shared_experience_of_absurdity/transcript?language=en.

Warner, Judith. *Perfect Madness: Motherhood in the Age of Anxiety*. New York: Riverhead Trade, 2005.

Wiens, Steve. "To Parents of Small Children: Let Me Be the One Who Says It Out Loud." *The Actual Pastor* blog. March 12, 2013. http://www.stevewiens.com/2013/03/12/to-parents-of-small-children-let-me-be-the-one-who-says-it-out-loud/.

Seuss, Dr. *The Lorax*. New York: Random House, 1971.

Stark, Roger. *The Waterfall Concept: A Blueprint for Addiction Recovery*. Brush Prairie, WA: Silver Star Publishing, 2010.

Uchtdorf, Dieter F. "The Love of God." October 2009. Transcript and video, 19:43. The Church of Jesus Christ of Latter-day Saints general conference. www.lds.org/general-conference/2009/10/the-love-of-god?lang=eng.

Van IJzendoorn, Marinus, Abraham Sagi, and Mirjam W. E. Lambermon. "The Multiple Caretaker Paradox: Data from Holland and Israel." In *Beyond the Parents: The Role of Other Adults in Children's Lives*. Edited by R. C. Pianta. San Francisco: Jossey-Bass, 1992.

Zak, Paul. "Trust, Morality—and Oxytocin?" Filmed July 2011. TEDGlobal, 16:34. https://www.ted.com/talks/paul_zak_trust_morality_and_oxytocin.

# About the Author

C. J. Schneider lives in Alberta, Canada, with her husband, three sweet children, a wild imagination, and a distaste for all things laundry. Though she had many adventures before motherhood—exploring and working in Asia, Europe, and Africa—her greatest and most challenging venture has been discovering the wonder of family and building a village of friends and fellow moms.

# About Familius

*Welcome to a place where parents are celebrated, not compared. Where heart is at the center of our families, and family at the center of our homes. Where boo-boos are still kissed, cake beaters are still licked, and mistakes are still okay. Welcome to a place where books—and family— are beautiful. Familius: a book publisher dedicated to helping families be happy.*

## Visit Our Website: www.familius.com

Our website is a different kind of place. Get inspired, read articles, discover books, watch videos, connect with our family experts, download books and apps and audiobooks, and along the way, discover how values and happy family life go together.

## Join Our Family

There are lots of ways to connect with us! Subscribe to our newsletters at www.familius.com to receive uplifting daily inspiration, essays from our Pater Familius, a free ebook every month, and the first word on special discounts and Familius news.

## Become an Expert

Familius authors and other established writers interested in helping families be happy are invited to join our family and contribute online content. If you have something important to say on the family, join our expert community by applying at:

**www.familius.com/apply-to-become-a-familius-expert**

## Get Bulk Discounts

If you feel a few friends and family might benefit from what you've read, let us know and we'll be happy to provide you with quantity discounts. Simply email us at orders@familius.com.

Website: www.familius.com

Facebook: www.facebook.com/paterfamilius

Twitter: @familiustalk, @paterfamilius1

Pinterest: www.pinterest.com/familius

---

The most important work you
ever do will be within the
walls of your own home.

---